BASEBALL BAFFLERS

by Wayne Stewart

Illustrated by Matt LaFleur

Sterling Publishing Co., Inc.
New York

I dedicate this book to all my buddies who have watched countless hours of baseball games with me and spent even more hours discussing the game: especially Rich Patch, Jack Haught, Paul and Mike Hanko, Kevin Zacovic, George Timko, and Pete Carbonaro.

Note: Some of the material in this book originally appeared in Beckett Publications and appears here with permission.

Edited by Claire Bazinet

Library of Congress Cataloging-in-Publication Data
Stewart, Wayne, 1951–
    Baseball Bafflers / by Wayne Stewart; illustrated by Matt Lafleur.
        p. cm.
    Includes index.
    ISBN 0-8069-6561-4
    1. Baseball–United States–Miscellanea. I. Title.
GV867.3 S84 1999
796.357'0973 21–dc21   99-044614

10 9 8 7 6 5 4 3 2

Published by Sterling Publishing Company, Inc.
387 Park Avenue South, New York, N.Y. 10016
© 1999 by Wayne Stewart
Distributed in Canada by Sterling Publishing
℅ Canadian Manda Group, One Atlantic Avenue,
Suite 105, Toronto, Ontario, Canada M6K 3E7
Distributed in Great Britain and Europe by Chris Lloyd
463 Ashley Road, Parkstone Poole, Dorset BH14 0AX, England
Distributed in Australia by Capricorn Link (Australia) Pty Ltd.
P.O. Box 6651, Baulkham Hills, Business Centre,
NSW 2153, Australia
Manufactured in the United States of America
All rights reserved

Sterling ISBN 0-8069-6561-4

Contents

Chapter

One	YOU'RE THE MANAGER	5
Two	YOU'RE THE UMPIRE	21
Three	STRANGE AND UNUSUAL PLAYS	31
Four	TRICK PLAYS	39
Five	WHO SAID IT?	53
Six	HAS IT EVER HAPPENED?	60
Seven	THE LIFE OF ROOKIES	66
Eight	LAST CHANCE TO PLAY MANAGER	81

Index   94

YOU'RE THE MANAGER

Baseball fans love to second-guess managers while they are watching a game. After all, part of the charm of the game is deciding what you would do if you were the manager.

Some fickle fans offer their opinions only after a negative outcome. For example, it isn't unusual to hear a spectator bellow, "I never would've stuck with that reliever," after the pitcher has just given up a home run. That second-guess scenario is all too familiar.

On the other hand, some knowledgeable fans will go out on a limb and declare their managerial intentions before a situation has run its course. This chapter affords you the opportunity to be a big league manager and make decisions based on real-life situations.

Read all the pertinent details about a given situation, then quickly make your move. Next, read on to learn what really happened or what most big league managers would've done in a certain situation.

Of course, the real-life job of managing entails more than just making calls. Consider the plight of Phil Cavarretta, manager of the Chicago Cubs for the 1954 season. As the team entered spring training, Cubs owner Phil Wrigley asked Cavarretta what the outlook was for the Cubs that year. Cavarretta made a serious mistake when he answered his boss honestly, reporting that things didn't look too bright.

Wrigley, who wanted optimism from his field generals, gave him the proverbial ax. Cavarretta became the first manager ever fired during spring training. Still want to be a big league manager? If so, read on and begin making your decisions.

Tough Call

Let's begin with a very difficult call, one that confronted San Diego Padres manager Preston Gomez back on July 21, 1970. His pitcher, Clay Kirby, was methodically mowing down the New York Mets. Through 8 innings, the Mets had not chalked up a hit.

Now comes the dilemma. Despite the no-hitter, Kirby was losing, 1–0. In the bottom of the eighth, the host Padres came to bat, and, with two men out, Kirby was due to hit. What did Gomez do? Did he pinch hit for Kirby in an effort to rev up some offense, or did he let Kirby remain in the game so the 22-year-old sophomore pitcher could try to secure his no-hitter?

What Happened

Gomez made a gutsy move that was criticized a great deal—he lifted Kirby for a pinch hitter. What really gave second-guessers ammunition for their anger was the fact that the move made no difference. The Padres went on to drop the game 3–0, and the bullpen went on to lose the no-hit bid. Through 1998, the Padres were one of just three teams (not counting 1998 expansion clubs) that had never recorded a no-hitter. (The others are the Mets and Rockies.)

Change of Scenario

If you voted emotionally to let Kirby try for the no-hitter and felt the choice was easy, you aren't alone—tons of fans feel this way. Now, however, let's change the scenario a bit. Would you remain as liberal if the game had entered the bottom of the ninth and was scoreless? Are you still sticking with him? Let's further assume Kirby is tiring a bit, and his pitch count is rapidly climbing.

Finally, for stubborn fans clinging to the thought of staying with Kirby, would it change your mind if you had a hot pinch hitter salivating, anxious to come off the bench? This time, there's no right or wrong answer—it's your call.

Similar Scenario

In 1974, the Houston Astros manager faced a situation much like the Clay Kirby near no-hitter. Don Wilson had worked his way through 8 innings of no-hit ball and was due up to bat in the 8th inning. The manager lifted Wilson for a pinch hitter. Moments later, the new pitcher, Mike Cosgrove, began the ninth by issuing a leadoff single to Cincinnati's Tony Perez for the only hit they'd get that day. The Reds also wound up winning the game, 2–1. The punch line here is that the Astros manager was none other than Preston Gomez.

Perhaps there's no connection, but Gomez managed Houston again in 1975 for part of the season (127 games), then went nearly five years before being hired again as a big league manager. After 90 games as the Cubs' manager, he never had a job as a major league skipper again.

Was Vida Feeling Blue?

Oakland A's manager Alvin Dark had a dilemma similar to Gomez's. On the final day of the 1975 season, Dark sent his ace, Vida Blue (with his 21 wins), to the mound. The A's had already clinched the Western Division, so Dark decided to have Blue pitch just 5 innings, then rest him for the upcoming playoffs.

At the end of those 5 innings, Blue had a no-hitter going. Dark didn't change his mind, though. He went to the bullpen for Glenn Abbott, who worked a hitless 6th inning. In the seventh, Dark brought in Paul Lindblad before turning the chores over to his closer, Rollie Fingers, to wrap it up. The quartet of pitchers managed to throw a highly unusual no-hitter with Blue getting the win. This game marked the first no-hitter by four men.

Intentional Walk Lunacy

Intentional walks are a big part of a manager's strategic repertoire. Frequently, with first base unoccupied, a team will deliberately walk a dangerous hitter and take its chances that the next batter will hit the ball on the ground. If he does and the defense turns a double play, a volatile situation is defused, and the team is out of a dangerous inning.

Would a situation ever call for intentionally walking a man with the bases loaded? As is the case with many of the plays that follow, this call is based on opinion. However, 99.99 percent of all the managers who ever filled out a lineup card would feel such a move was positive proof of temporary insanity. Believe it or not, such a move has taken place in a big league game, and on more than one occasion!

Two Intentional Incidents

The most recent occasion was on May 28, 1998, when the San Francisco Giants faced the Arizona Diamondbacks. The score was 8–6 in the bottom of the ninth. With two outs and the bases loaded, Arizona manager Buck Showalter ordered an intentional walk to the always-dangerous Barry Bonds.

After Bonds had moseyed down to first, the Giants were within one run. However, the next batter, Brent Mayne, made Showalter look good by lining out to right fielder Brent Brede on a payoff pitch, ending the contest.

The Second Bold Intentional Walk

Showalter wasn't the only manager who made a brazen strategic move in 1998. On May 24 in the 14th inning of a chaotic game, San Francisco manager Dusty Baker definitely went against accepted baseball wisdom. In the top of the 14th, with the game still tied, Giants pitcher Jim Poole handled St. Louis hitters Ron Gant and Delino DeShields with no problem. Mark

McGwire stepped up to the plate, and that's when it happened. Baker ordered an intentional walk to the hot-hitting Mark McGwire.

Baker was deliberately allowing the potential game-winning run to reach base. Traditionalists were apoplectic, but Baker had his reasons for the walk. First of all, anybody who followed the game in 1998 knew McGwire was one bad dude. In fact, he had already homered in the 12th inning. That gave him a major league-leading 24 blasts. With a full week to go in May, he was tied for the record for the most homers ever hit by the end of of that month. (Later, he did break that record.)

In addition, Baker was following the baseball adage that you just don't let certain superstars beat you—you take the bat out of their hands. On that day, Baker took McGwire's bat away three times with intentional walks.

When Ray Lankford followed with a single, things appeared to be shaky. However, Poole managed to strike out Willie McGee to end the inning without further damage. Ultimately, the move worked since the Giants went on to win 9–6 in 17 innings. Poole said of the walk, "Your first instinct is like, 'No!' Then you realize it's him [McGwire], and you say, 'Oh, well, I guess so.' He's going pretty good right now." Clearly that was an understatement.

Veteran pitcher Orel Hershiser captured the spirit of the event. He said, "Walk McGwire with nobody on? That's a legend. Jim Poole and Dusty Baker will be trivia, and McGwire will be the legend."

Walks from the Past

The last time prior to the Bonds bases-loaded intentional walk incident that such a tactic was used in the majors was on July 23, 1944, when the Giants player-manager, Mel Ott, faced the Cubs and Bill Nicholson. The Cubs strongman had homered three times in the first game of the twinbill, and wound up with six homers in the series by the time Ott made his unusual move. Nicholson's hot streak pushed him by Ott for the league leadership for homers. All this set the stage, and in the second game of a doubleheader at the Polo Grounds, Ott, with a 10–7 lead in the eighth inning, gave Nicholson (who represented the go-ahead run) a free pass with the bases loaded and two outs. Ott's logic was it's better to give up one run than four on a grand slam. For the record, the move worked, as the Giants held on to win, 12–10.

Legend has it that Hub Pruett walked Babe Ruth on purpose with the bases jammed on June 14, 1923, but reliable sources say this isn't true.

Nap Lajoie was actually the very first man to draw a bases-loaded intentional walk. On May 23, 1901, the White Sox led the Athletics 11–7 in the ninth, but with the bases loaded and nobody out, player-manager Clark Griffith left the bench and became the relief pitcher. At that point he decided to give the walk to Lajoie, who represented the tying run. Lajoie would hit over .400 that year, but had the bat taken out of his hands on that occasion. The decision to walk him paid off when Griffith got the next three batters. So, while the move is extremely rare, it has been done. Still, don't hold your breath waiting for the next time a manager pulls this tactic out of his cobwebbed bag of tricks.

Yet Another Unique Intentional Walk

Under any circumstances, would you walk the leadoff hitter if it meant putting the winning run on base or at the plate?

You probably shouldn't, but it has been done. Frank Howard, a star for the Los Angeles Dodgers and Washington Senators, couldn't recall specific names, but he stated, "I've seen a manager, against an especially hot hitter that could beat him in a tough ball game, intentionally walk him to lead off an inning, putting the winning run on base." Now that's a brazen move, folks.

Back to Ott

Ott, by the way, was no stranger to drawing walks. He drew five walks in a game four times during his career—a record that still stands. He also shares a record for coaxing seven straight walks over a three-day period in 1943. Additionally, from 1936 through 1942, he compiled 100-plus bases on balls, also an all-time big league record.

Then there was the time he drew six walks in a double-header. He was playing against the Phillies on October 5, 1929, and, as the season was winding down, he was shooting for the home run title. Chuck Klein of the Phillies was also trying to win that crown. So, Klein's manager, Burt Shooton, instructed his pitchers to pitch around Ott. Klein, in part thanks to the Shooton strategy, went on to lead the league in homers.

When *Not* Pitching Is Good

Along the same lines as the Ott intentional walk issue, sometimes not pitching to a slugger or a particularly hot hitter is as much a case of good strategy as, say, knowing when to yank a tiring pitcher from the hill.

In 1969, when San Francisco first baseman Willie McCovey was wielding a lethal bat, opposing managers avoided him as if he were a coiled, angry python. Not only did "Stretch" go on to win the National League's Most Valuable Player award (45 HR, 126 RBI, and a lofty .656 slugging percentage), he was awarded first base intentionally a record 45 times as well. That works out to about three intentional walks every 10 games.

Foxx Hunt

Consider, too, what American League managers did to Jimmie Foxx. During his 20-year career, spent almost entirely in the "Junior Circuit," Foxx amassed 534 homers, enough even now to rank in the all-time top ten. Knowing how powerful "Double X" was, managers often had their pitchers work around him.

On June 16, 1938, Foxx, by then with the Boston Red Sox, was well on his way to an incredibly productive season that included a .349 average, 50 home runs, and 175 runs batted in. On that day, the feared Foxx was issued six walks during a 9-inning game, still good for a major league record. While the walks were not officially listed as intentional walks, it's pretty obvious that pitchers worked him quite carefully. Again, *not* pitching can be a wise move.

To Pitch or Not to Pitch, That Is the Question

After all the talk about pitching or not pitching to blistering hot hitters, here's a real-life case. In the best-of-seven National League Championship Series (NLCS) back in 1985, the Los Angeles Dodgers squared off against the St. Louis Cardinals. The winner would head to the World Series.

The NLCS stood at 3 games to 2 in favor of the Cardinals. The Dodgers had to have a win. They were leading 5–4 as the top of the 9th inning rolled around. Then a critical situation developed. With two men out and runners on second and third, the Redbirds mounted a major threat. Even a single would probably score two, giving St. Louis the lead.

To make matters worse for the jittery Dodgers, the batter was Jack Clark, the Cardinals cleanup hitter, who had already crushed 22 homers and driven in 87 runs that year to go with his .281 batting average in just 126 games.

Other Factors

Clark, the right-handed first baseman, was 6 feet, 2 inches tall and weighed 205 pounds. Dodger manager Tommy Lasorda knew he could walk Clark since first base was open. That would set up a force play at every base and allow the bullpen to face the number-five hitter instead of Clark.

Lasorda had already decided he was sticking with his reliever Tom Niedenfuer. The big (6 feet, 5 inches; 225 pounds) righty had entered the game when starter Orel Hershiser got in a tough spot after recording just one out in a 3-run 7th inning for the Cards. Niedenfuer was 7–9 out of the bullpen. He had 19 saves and an earned run average of 2.71 on the season.

Lasorda's dilemma was to issue a walk to Clark or to have Niedenfuer go right at Clark to secure the final out.

Keep in mind three final bits of information: First, Niedenfuer had absorbed the loss in the fifth game of the NLCS just two days earlier. In that game, he had surrendered a 9th-inning game-winning home run to Ozzie Smith, of all people. Smith was just starting to shed his "good glove, no stick" label in 1985, but even then he had hit just six regular-season homers.

Second, the Dodger reliever had already whiffed Clark to help calm down a St. Louis uprising in the 7th inning. If he had Clark's number, it might be best to defy common strategic practice and pitch to Clark.

Third, if the Dodgers gave Clark a walk, the next batter they'd have to face would be a lefty, the 24-year-old outfielder Andy Van Slyke, coming off a .259, 13 home run, 55 RBI season. In such a situation, what would your call be?

The Actual Call and Results

Lasorda felt they could get Clark out. If your call was to walk Clark, you can gloat since Clark teed off on the very first pitch, jacking it out of the park for a pennant-winning home run. The Dodgers did have three outs left, but they were dead, going out one-two-three in the bottom of the ninth.

Incidentally, according to one version of this story, Lasorda instructed his reliever to pitch carefully to Clark, giving him an "unintentional-intentional walk." Still, a straightforward order for an intentional pass seems to have been the proper call.

While Lasorda's call took a lot of nerve, it also certainly went against the book. When you make such a call and things work out, you look like a genius. However, you wear the goat's horns when the call backfires.

To Hold or Not to Hold

Assume a runner is taking a lead off first base in a situation that seems to call for a stolen base. Also assume the runner does not possess the blazing speed of Brian Hunter, but he is a pretty good runner, definitely a threat to run, considering the game situation.

If your team is on defense, you might consider calling for a pitchout. You'd have the pitcher blister a high fastball way out of the strike zone, giving the catcher a ball he can handle easily. This strategy allows the catcher a great shot at gunning down the potential base burglar, especially since the pitchout gets the catcher out of his deep crouch.

Now, here's the question. Do you instruct your pitcher to hold the runner just a bit looser in such a situation? In other words, does the pitcher try not to tip off the runner that a play is on? In effect, does he encourage the man on first to run, almost enticing him, since you feel the catcher will fire the runner out. Is this wise?

Answer: Most managers would say you don't do anything special in this case. Rick Sutcliffe, winner of the Cy Young Award, once said, "You throw a normal pitch [a fastball with your normal delivery] to the plate. You glance at the runner with peripheral vision, but you do not hold him less closely."

According to Sutcliffe, the only thing that is different is that you don't throw over to the first baseman in an obvious attempt to hold the runner. So, you allow the runner his normal lead, but you make absolutely no pickoff moves when the pitchout is on. Pretty basic stuff, actually.

Ruth's World Series Larceny

It's the 9th inning of the seventh game of the 1926 World Series. Today's winner will be the new World Champion. The St. Louis Cardinals are leading the New York Yankees by a score of 3–2. You are the Yanks skipper, Miller Huggins, winner of 91 regular-season games.

Despite all that success, you are down to your last out. But all is not lost yet—Babe Ruth is on first base after drawing a walk. The game is still alive. If the "Bambino" could reach second base, he'd be in scoring position. A single could tie it up. Not only that, the batter now in the box is your cleanup hitter, Bob Meusel, and Lou Gehrig is on deck.

Meusel missed part of the season with a broken foot, but he still drove in 81 runs. Gehrig, meanwhile, had 83 extra base hits in 1926, his second full season in the majors. As for Ruth, he had swiped 11 bases during the season and was considered a pretty good base runner in his day.

Final Factors

The St. Louis pitcher was Grover Cleveland Alexander. Although he would come back in 1927 to post a stellar 21–10 record, the 39-year-old Alexander was on the downside of his career. He had pitched a complete-game victory just the day before our classic situation unfolded. Baseball lore states he had celebrated the win by going out on the town that evening …and into the morning. They say he didn't even witness the events prior to being called into the game because he was by then sleeping soundly in the bullpen.

Now, having worked flawlessly for 2 innings prior to the walk to Ruth, the game was on the line. He peered in to get the signal from his catcher, Bob O'Farrell, who had a .976 career fielding percentage.

Armed with all the data, what would you have done if you were in charge? Call for a hit-and-run play? Do nothing and let Meusel swing away? Have Meusel take a strike (not swing at a pitch until Alexander throws a strike)? This last would show whether Alexander was getting wild and/or tired; after all, he had just walked Ruth. Would you have Ruth steal to get into scoring position? Any other ideas?

What Happened

Ruth took his lead. Alexander fired a pitch, and Ruth, who had stolen a base the day before, took off for second. O'Farrell's throw beat Babe easily as St. Louis player-manager Rogers Hornsby applied the tag. The Series was over with the Yankees losing on a daring play that most experts felt was also a very foolish play.

Accounts of the game indicate that Huggins actually had Meusel hitting away and did not have Ruth running. The story goes that Ruth was running on his own, creating a terrible blunder. Few, if any, managers would have had Ruth running —it was way too risky.

Distraction

At the major league level, do managers and players employ tactics that work at the level of American Legion ball? Specifically, if you were a catcher, could you distract an opposing batter by pounding your mitt in an effort to trick him? The batter, hearing the sound coming from the mitt, can tell where the catcher is holding the glove. Presumably, he is telling the pitcher where he wants the pitch thrown.

The reality is that managers don't spend time teaching such tactics, but some players say you can distract or play mind games with your opponent. The story goes that one catcher used to toss dirt and pebbles into a batter's spikes to annoy him. Similarly, Yogi Berra was infamous for making small talk with a hitter in an effort to ruin his concentration. Remember when Hank Aaron responded to Berra's ploys by saying he was in the batter's box to hit, not chatter?

Mark Grace, an All-Star first baseman with the Chicago Cubs said, "Pounding the glove can work. It can distract you. It puts a thought in your mind. For example, the pitcher went inside with the last pitch, and the catcher is pounding the glove inside again. It can make you think. It's a mind game, but it doesn't stay in the mind too long." With a good hitter like Grace, once the pitch is on the way, such annoyances disappear, and the batter is set to hit.

Grace added that one thing that works for sure and is quite distracting is sheer intimidation. "It works for a pitcher," he stated. "That's what chin music is all about. A Nolan Ryan or a Dwight Gooden throws tight and sends a message: 'Don't dig in!'"

Speaking of Intimidation

Grace is correct. They sometimes call it the "art" of intimidation. Some of the greatest artists in that field were also among the game's greatest pitchers. If you were a major league manager, wouldn't you like to have some of the following characters on your staff?

- *Dizzy Dean.* Although he was considered a colorful guy, he could also get serious. Take the time he noticed a hitter digging in while settling into the batter's box. Dean glared at him, then bellowed in true Clint Eastwood "make my day" fashion, "You comfortable? Well, send for a groundskeeper and a shovel 'cause that's where they're going to bury you."

- *Nolan Ryan.* If he hit you with a pitch, you knew it would hurt. Jay Buhner, a bona fide slugger with the Seattle Mariners, once said of Ryan, "Nolan used to come up and stare you down."

- *Early Wynn.* He's supposed to have said that he'd knock down his own grandmother if she were crowding the plate, but that was probably apocryphal. However, Wynn was one fiery competitor.

- *Don Drysdale.* His philosophy of intimidation was quite simple: If the opposing team knocked down one of Drysdale's Dodger teammates, he'd knock down two of the opposing team's batters.

Clearly, the question about wanting such men on your staff is rhetorical. Nevertheless, intimidation is a very real, almost tangible part of baseball's hidden strategy.

Where Do You Bat Him?

Imagine you're at the helm of a pennant-winning team, and you're about to play the fourth game of the World Series. Would you consider batting your starting pitcher somewhere other than the traditional number-nine slot in the lineup?

Answer: You might, if the pitcher were George Herman Ruth. Babe Ruth left the ranks of pitchers after 1919, although he did pitch in five scattered contests after that. He became a pretty fair hitter, with a .342 lifetime batting average and 714 homers.

Actually, he was a fine hitter even while pitching—why do

you suppose his manager moved him to the outfield full-time? In the last two seasons in which he spent a significant time on the mound (1918 and 1919) he was used as an outfielder in 59 and 111 games respectively. He hit 11 homers in 1918, then 29 the following year. Both totals were good enough to lead the American League. He also drove in 66 runs, followed by 114 runs.

So, with all that in mind, it's not so shocking to learn that in 1918 (his 11-homer year), in his final Series outing as a pitcher, he hit in the sixth spot for the Boston Red Sox. This marked the only time in World Series history that a starting hurler appeared any place but ninth in the batting order.

The Outcome

The Sox skipper, Ed Barrow, made a good call. Although Ruth grounded out early in the game, he tripled-in two of Boston's three runs. In his final at-bat, he sacrificed. Meanwhile, the man who did hit in the ninth spot was a catcher by the name of Sam Agnew. He went 0-for-2 after hitting .166 on the year.

On the mound, Ruth worked 8 innings, got in trouble in the ninth, was relieved, then moved to the outfield as the Sox held on to win, 3–2. Boston also went on win the Series 4 games to 2. By the way, during this game, Ruth's streak of $29^{2}/_{3}$ consecutive scoreless innings (a record at the time) came to an end.

Quick Quiz

Do managers normally try to steal home in a situation like this? The runner on third can be anyone you choose. If you'd like, select Ty Cobb, who stole home an all-time record 50 times during his illustrious career. (Who wouldn't like that prospect?) Now, does it matter if the batter is a lefty or righty as long as you have the fiery Cobb barreling down the line as soon as the pitcher commits to throwing the ball to the plate?

Answer: Yes, it matters. Most managers feel they'd definitely prefer a right-handed batter in the box when they attempt a steal of home. Back in the 1940s, Jackie Robinson was known to have done it with a lefty in the batter's box, but he was special.

Incidentally, stealing home was rather common in the Cobb era, a dead-ball era in which you'd scratch for runs any way you could come by them.

Lately, swiping home is a rarity. Wade Boggs, a sure future Hall-of-Famer, says that nowadays you just don't see it done. "It's probably a lost art. Mostly it's done now with first and third. The guy on first takes off, then the guy on third takes off."

Nevertheless, when an attempt to steal home does occur, you still don't want a lefty at bat. A left-hander stands in the batter's box to the right of the catcher. Conversely, a right-handed hitter stands on the left side of the catcher.

What's the logic involved here? Kevin Stocker of the Tampa Bay Devil Rays explained, "If you're on the right side of the plate, and you're straight stealing, the catcher can see the runner coming and has no one to go around." In other words, there's nothing obstructing his tag.

Or, as Atlanta Braves manager Bobby Cox, perennial winner of division titles, put it, "You want the batter in the right hander's box to help block out the catcher." A righty obstructs the catcher's view of the runner dashing down the line. The catcher may not realize a play is on until it is too late to do anything about it.

There was once a runner who stole home standing up. This happened because the pitcher threw a pitch that was so wild, the catcher was only able to grab it after lunging out of the line of action. Thus, he couldn't even come close to tagging the runner.

Chapter Two

YOU'RE THE UMPIRE

Even fans who constantly boo the men in blue must realize how difficult their job is. To paraphrase a famous quote, umpiring is the only game where you must be perfect on your very first day on the job, then improve during the rest of your career.

This chapter provides you with the vicarious opportunity to become an umpire. You'll be presented with some facts, then you make the call. Good luck—you're probably about to learn that it isn't as easy as it looks.

Pickoff Chicanery

Say Ken Griffey, Jr. of the Seattle Mariners pounded a ball into the right field corner. The ball kicked around a bit, and Griffey kept digging around the base paths, sliding into third in a cloud of dust. Let's further imagine he called time-out to brush the dirt from his uniform.

Now the third baseman tosses the ball back to the pitcher, a righty. The pitcher straddles the rubber for a moment, then, seeing Griffey stroll off the bag, throws over. Griffey is doomed—or is he? You're the umpire. What's the call?

Answer: It is not an out; Griffey can stay at third base. In order for play to resume after a time-out, the pitcher must come in contact with the rubber, not merely straddle it. Thus, time is still out, and the play never happened.

Aaron and His 756 Homers

Every good fan knows Hank Aaron is the all-time home run king with 755 career blasts. But, here's a situation involving Aaron and home runs that many fans don't recall.

Back on August 18, 1965, in St. Louis, Aaron faced Cards pitcher Curt Simmons. Simmons lobbed a blooper pitch to Hammerin' Hank. The superstar right fielder slashed the ball on top of the pavilion roof at Sportsman's Park for a tape-measure blow. As Aaron stepped into the pitch, he actually wound up making contact with the ball while one foot was entirely out of the batter's box. Does this matter? Was Aaron permitted to trot around the bags with a home run, was it a "no pitch" call, or was he ruled out?

Answer: When a batter makes contact with a pitch while outside the box, he is declared out. Aaron would own 756 homers if it weren't for the sharp eyes of home plate ump Chris Pelekoudas.

When a Catch Is or Isn't a Catch

In 1991, Triple-A minor leaguer Rodney McCray was roaming the outfield for Louisville. On a long smash, McCray actually ran through a panel of the right field fence near the 369-foot marker. David Justice called this the most amazing thing he had ever seen on a diamond. Justice was in awe of McCray's courage. "At some point he had to know that he had been running for quite a long time." Bone-jarring impact was inevitable.

Clearly McCray made a spectacular catch, hauling the ball in on the dead run under those circumstances. Or did he make the catch? What's the ruling on this play? Is it illegal because he caught the ball but left the field of play because of his momentum?

The rule book states that, in order for a play to be a catch, the fielder has to have complete possession of the ball. In addition, the release of the ball must be voluntary, as opposed to, say, dropping the ball. Had McCray dropped the ball as a result of his impact with the fence, it would not have been a catch. As it was, the catch counted, and McCray became an instant hit on highlight films.

Great Catch

A similar play took place on May 3, 1998, in Three Rivers Stadium in Pittsburgh. Turner Ward of the Pirates pulled a "McCray" when he crashed through the right field wall after making his superb catch. Ward, who hurt his arm on the play, came back through the wall like a pro wrestler dramatically entering the ring. Then he short-armed the ball to a teammate.

Great Catch Nullified

Back in 1982, Terry Harper of the Atlanta Braves made a great catch that, due to an umpire's call, wasn't a catch. On September 26, in the middle of a pennant race, the Braves were playing the San Diego Padres. In the 3rd inning, San Diego's Gene Richards lofted a ball to left field. Harper speared the ball after making a long run. He caught the ball in fair territory, then crossed into foul territory.

Running as quickly as he was, he needed a good four long

strides to slow down. Those strides, though, put him in contact with a low bullpen railing. He grabbed at the railing to brace himself before tumbling into the bullpen area.

At about that time, he dropped the ball. Now the rule states that a ball that is dropped by a player immediately following contact with a wall is a live ball—no catch has been made. That's why umpire Ed Vargo ruled Harper's play a "no catch," and that's why the speedy Richards was able to cruise around the bases with an inside-the-park home run. To this day, Braves fans feel cheated by Vargo's interpretation that Harper hadn't held on to the ball long enough to validate the catch. They believe that the time that passed from the "catch" in fair territory until Harper hit the fence, including his many long steps holding on to the ball, were sufficient to prove it was a catch. Even an NBA official would've called Harper for traveling on this play, but the ump's call stands, as always.

Oldies but Goodies

Let's say you are umping a game back in 1919, and the batter is none other than the "Sultan of Swat," Babe Ruth. He drills a ball that flies by the foul pole in fair territory, then wraps around the pole before smacking into a seat in foul grounds. What's your call here—home run or merely a long, harmless foul ball?

This is a trick question. Today the ball is ruled fair. However, prior to 1920, such a play was called foul. The umpires judged the ball fair or foul by where it landed. Unlike Aaron and his "lost" home run, Babe Ruth didn't, in reality, lose any home runs because of this rule, but obviously some men did back then.

Little-Known Ground Rule

What happens if a fly ball clears a fence that is less than 250 feet from home plate? Although there is a rule prohibiting such a close fence in the major leagues, this could happen at the minor league level.

Answer: Due to an obscure 1926 rule, such a hit is automatically called a ground-rule double.

Another Tricky Oldie

The year is 1930, and the pitcher is Burleigh Grimes, a man who later retired with 270 career wins. Grimes goes to his mouth and loads up the baseball with a nasty concoction of chewing tobacco and saliva. If you were working that game, what would your call be?

Answer: Absolutely nothing. Although the spitball was outlawed in 1920, there was a grandfather clause that permitted a handful of pitchers to continue to throw their specialty pitch. The last man to legally throw a spitter was none other than Hall-of-Famer Burleigh "Ol' Stubblebeard" Grimes in 1934.

Sacrificial Players

Imagine that Bernie Williams of the Yankees is at the plate with a runner on third and nobody out. Williams powers the ball to deep left field where Barry Bonds races for the catch. Realizing the runner from third will easily score on the sacrifice fly, Bonds lets the ball hit his glove, but instead of securing the catch, he begins to bobble the ball. In a weird sort of juggling act, he continues to bounce the ball in and out of his glove while running towards the plate.

When he finally gets to very shallow left field, nearing the shortstop position, he lets the ball settle into his glove. The runner from third knows he can't tag up now, and he stays at third. Is the Bonds trick legal?

What Bonds did will count as a legal catch. The runner from third, though, was foolish. The rules say you can tag up the moment the ball touches the fielder's glove, not when it is actually caught. If this play really had happened, both the runner and third base coach would have been ripped by the manager and the media as well.

More on Sac Flies

In *Baseball Oddities*, I discussed another trick play involving sacrifice flies. Veteran catcher Don Slaught said that if a fly ball is hit to an outfielder when there are fewer than two outs and there is a man on third, "He has to pretend to catch it like he normally does, then basket-catch it. Then if the guy [the runner on third] takes off just a tad too early, maybe we can catch him." If so, it would be a legal play, and the runner would be out for leaving early.

Quick Quiz

Here are umpiring situations that come up from time to time. You make the quick calls on these relatively simple situations.

1) A ball is rolling in foul territory between home plate and first base. Before a fielder touches it, the ball hits a pebble and rolls back into fair ground where it comes to a stop. Fair or foul?

2) Roberto Alomar hits a Baltimore chop; the ball hits home plate before it takes its first high hop. He beats the play out at first. Is this a single or a foul ball for hitting the plate?

3) A grounder trickles through the right side of the infield, just inside the first base line. It barely eludes Will Clark of the Texas Rangers. In frustration Clark turns, takes off his mitt, and fires the glove at the ball. The mitt strikes the glove, causing it to roll foul near the right field stands. Make your call.

Answers:

1) The ball is fair. The decision depends on where the ball comes to a halt. On slow-moving balls in foul territory, fielders always hustle to touch the ball before it can roll back into fair territory. This kills the play, avoiding a cheap single.

2) Contrary to what many fans believe, the plate is in fair territory—give Alomar a hit.

3) The penalty for hitting a fair ball with a thrown glove is three bases for the batter. Any runners on board at the time also are awarded three bases. If Clark's mitt had struck a thrown ball, the punishment would have been two bases.

Follow the Bouncing Ball

On May 26, 1993, as Texas was playing the Cleveland Indians, a long fly ball off the bat of Carlos Martinez headed towards Jose Canseco. The not-so-hot-with-the-glove Canseco caught up to the ball, but he didn't catch it. In fact, the ball actually hit him on the head before soaring over the right field fence. Was it a ground-rule double or a homer?

The umpires that day ruled correctly that it was a (highly embarrassing) home run.

Monday, Monday

On May 10, 1977, the Montreal Expos were at home facing the Los Angles Dodgers. Warren Cromartie tattooed a long drive to center field. Rick Monday gave chase. Although he got close to the ball, it struck the wall over his head. Then it ricocheted off the wall, cracked Monday on his forehead, and rebounded over the wall. Is this play basically the same as Canseco's, or does the fact that it first bounced off the wall change things? What do you award Cromartie?

Answer: Once it hit the wall, it was considered to be a "bounding ball." Such plays result in a ground-rule double, not a home run.

More Bounces

Back in 1993, Damon Buford was in the Orioles batter's box facing pitcher Matt Young. A pitch to Buford hit the ground and bounced up towards the plate. Buford didn't care that it one-hopped its way to the strike zone; he swung and hit a comebacker to Young. When Young lobbed the ball to first, Buford was ruled out. Did the umpire blow this call? Should it have been a dead ball and no pitch?

Answer: The call was correct. Herb Score, a 20-game winner in 1956, said he once "threw one up to the plate that bounced, and the batter swung and hit a home run." Even if a batter is hit by a pitch that hits the dirt first, it counts. Such a runner would be given first base.

Little League Call

Kids and even some Little League umpires seem to foul up the next situation. Let's say a batter hits a grounder to short-stop. The hitter beats the play out by a half step. His momentum carries him several strides down the right field line. He then makes a slow turn to his left, towards second base. The first baseman is still holding the ball. Seeing the runner make his little turn, the first baseman tags the runner, claiming that if you veer at all towards second base you are in effect running there, giving up your right to saunter safely back to first base. Is the defensive player correct in his logic?

No. This is a common fallacy of baseball. It doesn't matter which way the runner turns when coming back to first base as described. The only time you can tag out the runner is when he turns to his left and makes an actual attempt to go to second.

Penalty for Suffering Pain?

Mo Vaughn is known for crowding home plate. He even wears a special protective device on his right arm. What would happen if the big first baseman were hit by a pitch on an 0–2 delivery as he was swinging at the ball?

Answer: It's a strikeout, and any runners on base must freeze. The ball is dead, so they can't advance.

Another Hit-by-Pitch Scenario

Must a batter make a legitimate effort to avoid getting hit by the ball, or is the fact that he was hit sufficient to earn a free trip to first base?

Answer: The batter must try to dodge the pitch. Perhaps the most famous case involving this rule occurred in 1968. Don Drysdale, Los Angeles's standout right-hander, was in the midst of a fantastic streak of shutout innings.

In a game versus the Giants, he faced a bases-loaded, no-outs situation. Dick Dietz, the San Francisco catcher, was at the plate with a 2-and-2 count. Drysdale came in tight with a pitch that hit him. Dietz got ready to stroll to first base, forcing in a run.

But wait a minute—home plate umpire Harry Wendelstedt ruled that Dietz had made no move to avoid the pitch. Despite an argument that raged on and on, the ruling stood, and the pitch was ball three.

When Dietz proceeded to fly out, Drysdale's shutout streak continued, eventually stretching to 58$\frac{2}{3}$ innings. Incidentally, that record was later broken by another Dodger, Orel Hershiser.

The Waiting Game

With no runners on base, Angels fireballing reliever Troy Percival came into a game to face the Baltimore Orioles. Percival, in a less dramatic version of Al "The Mad Hungarian" Hrabosky, went behind the mound to gather his thoughts. The home plate umpire timed Percival, said he violated a delay of game rule, and called an automatic ball on him. Can this happen?

Yes. The rule states that with no men on base, a pitcher has just 20 seconds to deliver a pitch. Thus, the relief pitcher was behind in the count, 1-and-0, before even throwing a pitch.

The umpires probably invoked this little-known rule because Percival is notorious for such tactics. The Orioles manager, Ray Miller, said of the relief pitcher, "This guy warms up, nervous as hell, walks around the mound, says prayers, bows behind the mound, looks over the center field fence, and everything else. They got tired of it and called ball one."

More Delays

Albert Belle, Baltimore's volatile slugger is at the plate. Let's say he gets irate over a strike call you, the umpire, just made. He starts to jaw with you. After a few moments, you get fed up with the delay and tell Belle to get in the box and quit squawking. What do you do if Belle refuses to obey your orders?

In this case, you would order the man on the mound to pitch the ball. As a punishment, you would call that pitch a strike even if it isn't in the strike zone. In addition, if the batter still refuses to step in and face the pitcher, every subsequent pitch is ruled a strike until the recalcitrant batter whiffs.

In real life, this happened to Frank Robinson after he argued about a called strike two. Moments later, the umpire called strike three, and the future Hall-of-Famer had lost the battle and the war.

Chapter Three

STRANGE AND
UNUSUAL PLAYS

Baseball has produced some extremely unusual plays over the years. As you'll soon read, there are tales of two men stealing four bases on one pitch and of hidden balls that aren't a part of the old hidden ball trick. No doubt about it, strange plays can be baffling, intriguing, and amusing. Clearly, they are also an important factor in the charm of baseball.

When a Non-Pitcher Threw a Spitball

You'd expect a spitball to be a saliva-drenched pitch thrown from the mound by, say, a Gaylord Perry. True enough, but once a first baseman was actually guilty of loading up a ball.

The rule book says, "[A] pitcher shall not bring his pitching hand in contact with his mouth or lips while in the 18-foot circle surrounding the pitching rubber." A strange play relating to this rule ensued when Rusty Staub, then playing first base for the Houston Astros, approached the mound to settle down pitcher Larry Dierker.

Staub asked for the ball. Dierker, now the Astros manager, handed it to him. Staub spit on the ball and rubbed it while chatting with Dierker. When he saw Staub applying the drool to the ball, umpire Shag Crawford declared an automatic ball as punishment. Since the count on the hitter was 3-and-1 at the time, Staub caused a walk because he had loaded up the ball!

When a Non-Pitcher Committed a Balk

In May of 1984, Jerry Remy was playing second base for the Boston Red Sox when he caused a balk. Not only that, he did it without even touching the ball!

Here is how it happened: Marty Castillo of the Detroit Tigers had just doubled. The Sox felt he had missed first base and were about to make an appeal play. Remy thought there was a chance that the Boston pitcher, lefty Bruce Hurst, would overthrow the ball. Since it never hurts to back up a play, Remy positioned himself behind first base in foul ground.

Although the appeal was denied, a strange play resulted. The Tigers requested a balk call because Remy's actions, they argued, violated Rule 4.02, which states that all players other than the catcher must be in fair territory when a ball is in play. The umpires agreed with the Tigers' contention and charged Hurst with a bizarre balk. That's a clear case of an almost-innocent bystander being victimized. Ultimately though, according to the rules, Hurst must take the responsibility.

An Easy Homer

On July 1, 1997, the Astrodome was the site of yet another crazy play. The Houston Astros were playing the Cleveland Indians. Normally these two teams would never meet during the regular season because they are in different leagues. However, due to the interleague play that season, they were squaring off.

Each park has its own ground rules, so players need to know the quirks of the ballpark. Not knowing such rules cost the Indians a home run. Manny Ramirez, often accused of having a short attention span, was in right field when a Tim Bogar bouncer rolled down the first base line. Ramirez saw the ball come to rest under the Houston bullpen bench, and he waved to an umpire that the ball was out of play.

The only problem was that the bench was, in fact, in play. First base umpire Charlie Reliford gestured that the ball was still alive. Ramirez's hesitation and lack of knowledge gave

Bogar time to circle the bases with an easy inside-the-park home run.

Little League Play

Some plays that work on a lower level of baseball simply don't work at the major league level—or at least they shouldn't work. Still, with the right ingredients, anything goes. For example, on May 12, 1998, the Pittsburgh Pirates were playing the Colorado Rockies. Kirt Manwaring laced a ball into right field for an apparent single. Pittsburgh right fielder Jose Guillen came up with the ball quickly and rifled it to first base. Embarrassingly, Manwaring was gunned out. Later, he likened the experience to the feeling you get in a dream where you run as hard as you can, but you don't move at all.

The play worked because of four factors. First, Manwaring, a catcher, is slow-footed. Second, the ball got to Guillen in a hurry. Third, Guillen fielded the ball quickly, charging in to make the play. Finally, Guillen's arm resembles Roberto Clemente's—it's that good.

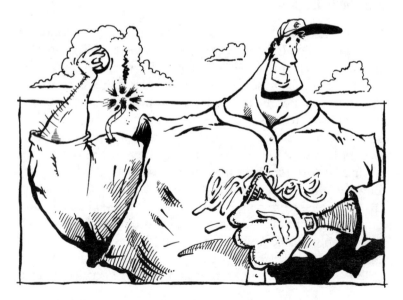

More Embarrassment

In 1993, Tom Candiotti was on the mound for the Los Angeles Dodgers when a runner took off for second, attempting a steal. Mike Piazza, who was a rookie catcher that year, came up gunning the ball. The throw was on line, but it never reached second because it struck Candiotti in his derriere.

The knuckleball pitcher later said, "I couldn't help but laugh at that one. I've dodged line drives before, but never a throw from a catcher."

Hit Your Cutoff Man

When Dave Winfield was with the San Diego Padres, he once went through a bad stretch of games in which he had difficulty hitting his cutoff man.

Shortly after a workout focusing on hitting cutoffs, Winfield had a chance to snap out of his defensive woes. On a hard-hit single to the outfield, Winfield quickly and smoothly came up with the ball in shallow center field.

Darrell Thomas lined himself up with Winfield to take the throw. But, since he saw Winfield was very close to the infield, Thomas knew the strong-armed outfielder would not need him for a relay throw. So Thomas ducked and spun around to watch the play at the plate.

Meanwhile, Winfield's throw came in hard, low, and right on target for the relay man. The ball hit Thomas directly on his backside, much like the Candiotti scenario.

After the game Winfield joked, "I finally hit the cutoff man."

Wrong-Way Corrigan Act

Sid Fernandez inexplicably performed a Wrong-Way Corrigan act back on August 20, 1990. At that time, the lefty pitcher was with the New York Mets. He came to the plate with a man on base and laid down a sacrifice bunt. Then came the chaos. For some reason, Fernandez trotted towards third base.

After a moment he realized his blunder, but it was too late. San Diego not only got a force-out on the runner, they also turned a double play on the disoriented pitcher. It was almost as if he had a momentary case of baseball dyslexia.

A Mickey Mantle Tale

Longtime Detroit Tiger announcer Ernie Harwell recalled what had to be one of the longest singles in the history of the game. He said, "I saw Mickey Mantle hit a ball that bounced into the center field bleachers at Yankee Stadium. He hit it with the bases loaded in an extra-inning game.

"At first, they gave him a ground-rule double, then they looked it up and could only award him a single." According to the rule book, the batter is awarded a single since it only took a single to drive in the run from third. The only exception to this rule is a game-winning home run. In that situation, they do not take away the homer even if a lesser hit would have won the game (as was the case with Mantle).

"Hidden" Ball Play

On July 1, 1998, the Chicago White Sox were playing the Houston Astros when, in a weird variation on the old "hidden" ball play, an umpire, not a player, "hid" the ball. Doug Henry was on the mound for Houston, and the Sox had Ray Durham on third.

Atlanta Braves coach Pat Corrales picks up the play-by-play from there: "It looked like the pitch was a sinker, and it hit the ground and bounced up. The ball got by the catcher and went in the umpire's [front] pocket and got buried there.

"The hitter didn't know where it was, the catcher didn't know, and the umpire [Gerry Davis] didn't know. The runner crossed the plate, then everybody realized where the ball was."

Durham scored easily as the befuddled catcher, Brad Ausmus, was the loser in this zany game of hide-and-seek. In reality, according to baseball rules, once the ball was "lost," it was also, in medical terminology, DOA. And once a ball is declared dead, searching for it was pointless. As Corrales pointed out, "If it gets stuck like that, you get one base, once they figured out where the ball was." He called it one of the strangest things he'd ever seen in the majors.

Running Wild

Most fans love to watch displays of power. Many fans also enjoy the speed game in baseball. Getting a chance to see a Lou Brock blaze around the bases is a thrill. One of the craziest plays involving speedy runners took place in 1985 when the Chicago Cubs hosted the St. Louis Cardinals.

With Vince Coleman on second and Willie McGee on first, the Cards put on the double steal. Coleman stole third easily, but he ran so rapidly that he slid past the bag. Realizing he couldn't get back to third without being tagged, he jumped up and dashed towards home plate.

Meanwhile, the fleet-footed McGee, who was on second, saw what had occurred and scampered for third. Amazingly, Coleman made it home, and McGee went into third unscathed. The end result was, due to a unique scorer's decision, four stolen bases on one pitch!

E, E, E

Don Slaught calls the next play one of the funniest moments he ever saw on a diamond. It was funny in two ways. It was "odd" funny; and it was also "gallows humor" funny.

Slaught, the catcher that day, relates which happened on July 27, 1988: "I was in New York with the Yankees when Tommy John had...three errors on one play. I think the ball was hit back to him; and he bobbled it for an error, then threw it wild to first for another error. The right fielder [Dave Winfield] caught the ball, threw it in. John cut if off, wheeled and threw it to me, but [he] threw it in the dugout for his third error on one play."

That play made John the first pitcher in the modern era to be guilty of three errors in an inning, and he did it all in a matter of seconds on one zany play.

A Not-So-Grand Slam

Cesar Cedeño of the Houston Astros hit what has to be one of the strangest hits, and perhaps the shortest grand slam ever. It happened on September 2, 1971, when Cedeño hit a 200-foot flyball with the bases loaded. Two Dodgers, second baseman Jim Lefebvre and right fielder Bill Buckner, converged on the ball.

They collided, and the ball fell in safely. By the time the Dodger defense could come up with the ball, it was too late. Cedeño had already circled the bases with a rather tainted grand slam.

More Inside-the-Park Wildness

On July 25, 1998, Turner Ward came to the plate as a pinch hitter for the Pittsburgh Pirates. He faced Dennis Martinez. What followed was about as bizarre as it gets. He hit the ball down off the plate, causing it to resemble a kid on a pogo stick, bouncing up the middle.

Atlanta Braves second baseman Tony Graffanino got to the ball, but he was only able to get a glove on it. That caused the ball to change directions, caroming past center-fielder Andruw Jones. Reportedly, Jones didn't hustle after the ball when it got by him, and Ward waltzed home with a strange inside-the-park homer.

Chapter Four

TRICK PLAYS

This section of the book includes some unusual trick plays including two unique hit-and-run plays. We won't argue semantics about the hit-and-runs being trick plays, since they are, in fact, standard plays, but ours have a most unusual twist. If you were running a team, do you think you'd be willing to try some of these plays?

Earl Weaver's Favorite

Outfielder Al Bumbry was a catalyst for manager Earl Weaver for many years with the Baltimore Orioles. Bumbry spoke fondly of a trick play they used to run. With a lefty on the mound and runners on first and third, the Orioles would wait for the pitcher to check the runners.

Bumbry said, "When the pitcher would look back to first, the guy on first would break [or take a big enough lead that he could get picked off on purpose]. When he broke, then the guy on third would break." Since the runner from first went before the pitcher had begun his delivery, the runner appeared to be an easy prey. Thus, the runner from third was often overlooked. When executed properly, the runner from third actually began to run before the pitcher made his pickoff throw to first.

Bumbry smiled. "Earl loved it. We ran it two times in one game against one particular pitcher; it worked. Earl would pick the right spot, and you had to pick the right pitcher, too. There were several elements he'd look for, but generally [the play was used against] one of the nonathletic pitchers, particularly lefties, and a guy who didn't have a very good move. Often it was a big left-hander who had a big delivery to the plate."

Weaver would run it with a righty on the mound, too, but with a slight variation. The runner off first draws a throw, then gets involved in a run down. The key difference here is that the runner from third won't go until the pitcher starts his move to first.

Larry Rothschild, manager of the Tampa Bay Devil Rays, also remembered the play. He said, "Billy Martin did that, too —the 'forced balk,' trying to draw a throw from the pitcher, and then the guy from third scores, or the pitcher balks.

"They do that with a left-hander because [working out of the stretch position] he can see the runner off first [and thus get duped into throwing there]. You're trying to steal home is what you're doing in a different way.

"Sometimes," added Rothschild, "the runner stumbles a little bit [on purpose] so the pitcher really thinks he can pick him off. The second that throw's made, the runner [off third] takes off."

Don Zimmer and the Book

In baseball terminology, if a manager "plays it by the book," he is determining his strategy based on what is considered to be accepted, normal practices. For example, bringing a left-handed relief pitcher into the game in a key situation against a left-handed batter is the usual practice for managers in this oversimplified scenario.

Don Zimmer has built a reputation for being willing to veer away from the routine path on occasion. The gutsy Zimmer has been around the major leagues as a player, coach, and manager since 1954. In 1998, he wore jersey number 50 to celebrate his total of fifty years in organized pro ball. Nicknamed "Popeye" for his facial appearance, he has experienced success at every level of play. In 1996 and 1998, for example, he was Joe Torre's bench coach when the Yankees won the World Series. In 1989, he steered the Cubs to a rare title, capturing the National League's Eastern Division.

Chris Chambliss, a Yankee coach in 1998, said, "As far as somebody who's not afraid to try things, Zim is really the best man to talk to. He's a gambling kind of guy."

Now, your question: Would you, under any circumstances, employ the hit-and-run with the bases loaded?

Most big league managers would probably give you an an emphatic "NO!" If your name is Zimmer, however, the answer is a qualified yes. If the situation were right, Zimmer would call for the hit-and-run with the bases full.

Since Chambliss said that Zim is the best man to talk to, we did just that. Zimmer explained how and why he pulled such a "crazy" play: "The first time I did it was with Bob Montgomery in Boston. I mean, you've got to have everything right to even think of doing it.

"I happened to have a sinkerball pitcher pitching against us, and Montgomery was a slow runner, but a pretty good bat handler, and I didn't think he could strike Montgomery out. And I didn't want Montgomery to hit a ground ball because he's slow, and any ground ball that he hit that a fielder could catch is a double play. So it just struck me—play hit-and-run. I did this maybe four or five times in the major leagues."

He seems surprised the play has been so widely discussed. "If you think about it, and when I explain it, it doesn't become that big. You got men on first and second and one out or no outs, and the count goes 3-and-2 on the hitter. Nine out of ten times, the runners are running." Now, extending that logic, why not let three men run with bases loaded?

Zimmer feels those two plays are similar, so he would hit-and-run with the bases loaded. The advantage is that if the slow-running hitter hits it on the ground versus the sinkerball pitcher, you'll score a run and avoid the double play. On the negative side, a line drive or strikeout can result in a double or triple play, but that's also true of the hit-and-run with first and second occupied. In addition, with the sinkerball pitcher, you're more likely to hit a ground ball than a line drive. So, as Joe Torre said of this play, "With a contact hitter at the plate, why just sit back and wait for the double play?"

Buck Rodgers Concurs

Buck Rodgers, an admiring managerial peer of Zimmer, agreed that the situation would have to include certain favorable factors. Rodgers, who managed against Zimmer in the National League East when he was with the Montreal Expos, pointed out three vital elements: "A batter at the plate who usually makes good contact, a pitcher who has good control and is usually around the plate with his pitches, and a pitcher who isn't a big strikeout pitcher."

Furthermore, the count on the batter would have to be one that would require the pitcher to come in with a strike—a count of 3-and-1, for example.

Dwight Gooden remembered a time Zimmer pulled off this trick: "One year when Zimmer was with the Cubs, with less than two outs, he sent everybody. It was the hit-and-run with the bases loaded. Lloyd McClendon was the hitter. I'd never seen that. It worked," Gooden marveled with a grin.

Such moves don't always pay off, of course. Rafael Palmeiro said, "I remember when [Zimmer] was the manager of the Cubs. I was playing…in '88, and we had the bases loaded in New York against the Mets. Manny Trillo was the batter, and the count was 3-and-2, I believe, when Zimmer put the hit-and-run on. Trillo swung through a pitch up in the zone, and Gary Carter caught the ball and tagged the runner for a double play, and we were out of the inning."

Another longtime baseball man, Johnny Goryl (who once was traded for Zimmer), said, "Zimmer is the kind of a guy who would use [unusual plays] to get an edge on you. Being a student of the game and knowing his players, he would do something like that."

Two More Men's Thoughts

Finally, on the topic of the bases loaded hit-and-run, the thoughts of yet another manager, Larry Rothschild: "I think Don Baylor did it in Colorado a couple of times [this would make sense since Zimmer served as Baylor's bench coach from 1993 to 1995]. You don't see that—the odds of it backfiring and costing you dearly are too great.

"I don't think that's having guts [to run such a play]. I think it's [a matter of] intelligence." Rothschild did concede that it depends on whether a manager such as Baylor has the right situation. "It's more of a calculated risk. If it works, great. If it doesn't, you really screwed up."

Bobby Cox disagrees. "There's nothing wrong with that strategy. Why not try something. I like that type of stuff. There's no 'book.'" He added, "It's a lot more fun." Of course, being with the successful Braves, Cox could afford to try any kind of play.

Sparky's Hit-and-Run

Another legendary manager who employed unorthodox plays at times was Sparky Anderson. Travis Fryman, who played for Anderson, said the only two men he could think of who used unique plays such as a hit-and-run with a man on third were Zimmer and Anderson.

Johnny Goryl said of Anderson, "He'd put on a hit-and-run with a runner on third so the runner could score on a ground ball. The disadvantage is if the hitter misses the ball, you're 'out to lunch,' or you could have a line-drive double play.

"The situation has to be with a contact hitter at the plate who'll put the ball in play on the ground," stated the longtime coach and manager. "Of course the count must also be favorable to the hitter—a count where the pitcher is going to throw a strike."

Frank Howard summed up the play: "What they're really doing is, rather than wait for contact to be made before you start the runner at third base, he's getting his runner in motion in case contact is made on the ground." And, if that contact is made, says Howard, "It's a walk home."

In Theory, That Is

What Howard and Goryl said makes sense, but sometimes a play gets botched. Listen to former Detroit Tiger catcher John Flaherty, who didn't execute the play. "I was playing for Sparky Anderson in 1995, and he put a hit-and-run on with a man on third, a 2-and-1 count, and the infield was in. Of course, I thought I missed the sign, so I stepped out and asked him to go through it again, and they took off the play.

"He let me know after that inning that, for him, all I had to do was put the ball in play and get an easy RBI. So that's why he put the sign on. But I've never seen anybody do that ever before, so it caught me by surprise.

"He did [that play] pretty much with just me, a light-hitting catcher. Just try to put the ball in play—that was the only time it ever came up, though," he observed.

Flaherty was asked if that play is similar to the contact play, and if, with the infield in, it gives the offense a head start with a grounder. He replied, "Exactly. For me, somebody who doesn't run that well and didn't have a lot of power at the time, he thought it was a good opportunity to get an easy run early in the game. But you don't see it very often." Nor, he could have added, will you see it much if players miss the sign because of their incredulity.

Orioles manager Ray Miller has another name to add to the list of innovative managers: "I saw Warren Spahn when he used to manage in the minor leagues. He used to hit-and-run with a man on third all the time. It's not a real envious position for the baserunner coming down the line, and a guy's swinging, but it was different."

Torre's Temptation

Joe Torre's Yankees were so hot in 1998, he didn't need to try trick plays. He seems to side with his coach, Chris Chambliss, who said, "There's really no reason to try to reinvent baseball. You want to stay within the basic framework of the game." Torre noted: "Some of those strategies like Zimmer's, I just don't have the courage to do."

However, Torre did say there is one play that he's tempted to try. "I'm gonna have the guts to do this one day if we're fortunate to continue to play the way we are. I may, in a lefty–righty situation, have a left-handed pitcher in the game, and he gets a left-hander [batter] out. Then I stick him at first base for an out [bringing in a bullpen righty to pitch to a right-handed hitter, playing the percentages], then bring the lefty back in.

"I think that's fascinating, and I admire the managers who have the courage to do it. I haven't had the courage yet. I'm just afraid something bad's gonna happen."

In the past, managers have made this move. It's believed to have originated with Paul Richards, who placed southpaw starting pitcher Billy Pierce at first base while reliever Harry Dorish retired a righty. After getting the out, Pierce would resume pitching.

Johnny Goryl remembered other managers who would "try to hide a pitcher out there in the outfield, then bring him back in [to pitch as Torre described]." Two other pitchers come to mind who did this: "Sudden" Sam McDowell, a southpaw for the Cleveland Indians, and Kent Tekulve, a right-handed reliever for the Pirates.

Goryl continued, "Back in those days, we only had eight- or nine-man pitching staffs, ten was the most clubs carried. Today we've got thirteen-man staffs, so you don't see this much...now."

Corrales Comments

Ask ten experts about trick plays, and you'll surely get ten different replies. In a 1998 interview, Pat Corrales pretty much agreed with Chambliss: "There aren't too many tricks to baseball other than pickoffs and stuff. The Japanese probably have more tricks than anybody, but a lot of times those things will work more against you than for you. That's the reason we [Atlanta] don't have them." Like Chambliss and the Yankees, who were on a record-setting pace for victories, the Braves, by and large, stick to the basics.

Cheating, Baseball Style

The next trick play calls for speed, guts, and even a wee bit of cheating (which in baseball is sometimes called being crafty). Kevin Stocker described the play: "It's the old double squeeze," he began. "Guys on second and third, and you squeeze bunt and keep the guy from second going. A lot of times we used to run that play [on an amateur level]. I think we may have even done it in the minor leagues.

"When the runners take off on the pitcher, the batter squeezes to the third baseman, and the runner from second cuts the bag at third—he doesn't actually touch the bag. He kinda cuts in front to steal a little time and hopes to catch the umpire sleeping. And it used to work quite a bit. It could work in college, but not so much at this level," he concluded.

The key is that the runner from second never hesitates as the other team goes for the out at first on the bunter. Then, as Stocker says, "You hopefully beat the throw going from first to home." When you succeed here, you get two runs for one little bunt, just one mere out.

Hidden Ball, Part I

On September 19, 1997, Matt Williams was playing third base for the Indians against the Kansas City Royals. In the 1st inning, he decided to try the hidden ball trick. According to Sandy Alomar, "He told the guy [base runner Jed Hansen] to get off the base so he could clean it. He was a rookie. Williams tagged the guy, and he was out. They were pretty upset about that." The Royals were so upset, in fact, that when Williams came to the plate in the next inning, no one was shocked to see him hit by a pitch. Starting pitcher Ricky Bones plunked him with a fastball, nearly starting a fight.

The trick play had actually begun when the Royals' second baseman stole third and began chatting with his third base coach, Rich Dauer. At that point, Williams made his house-cleaning request, which the rookie unbelievably obeyed. "I was gullible enough to step off. It took me totally by surprise. I was not paying attention. It won't happen again," said the 25-year-old victim.

Williams explained how the play went: "It was sort of a spur-of-the-moment thing. I wasn't trying to embarrass any-one." Williams had taken the throw on the steal from catcher Pat Borders. He then made a motion as if he were lobbing the ball back to pitcher Brian Anderson. Williams actually tossed the ball into his own glove. His next move was to show the hidden ball to the umpire to alert him as to what was about to happen.

Williams, who had spent his entire career in the National League prior to 1997, was worried, "I've noticed that the umpires in this league call time-out a lot." If the ump had done that, the play would have been dead right there. As it was, Anderson almost blew it by gawking over at Williams.

Coach Goryl marveled, "He did a helluva job with it. That was the first time I saw it done in the big leagues in a long time."

Hidden Ball, Part II

Having succeeded in pulling off the hidden ball trick in 1997, Williams tried it again early in 1998, on April 2—perhaps as a belated April Fools' Day trick. Williams probably picks his targets depending upon their inexperience, since this time he went after 22-year-old Neifi Perez. While Perez technically was not a rookie, he had barely over one-tenth of a year of major league service to his credit.

Perez tripled to lead off the 9th inning for the Colorado Rockies. Williams, by then with Arizona, acted as if he were giving the ball to Diamondback pitcher Felix Rodriguez, who was standing near third base.

Ironically, it was the rookie pitcher who botched the play due to his inexperience. Rodriguez went to the rubber without the ball and was called for a balk.

More Hidden Ball Info

Goryl said that Tim Ireland, a minor-leaguer, was the best player he ever saw at executing this trick. Goryl stated that in one year at the Double-A level, Ireland caught as many as nine guys sleeping. "He was lucky nobody punched his lights out," said Goryl. Ireland would hide the ball by sneaking it under his left armpit. He'd then stand near the runner while jabbing the pocket of his mitt with his fist to lull the runner into believing Ireland did not have the ball. When the runner took a lead, Ireland would retrieve the ball and tag him out.

Another way a fielder once hid the ball was by walking over to the pitcher and plopping the ball into the pitcher's glove.

He did this in clear sight of the runner. However, like a magician, he also performed some sleight of hand. Quicker than the eye of the runner could see, the fielder had slipped his own glove inside the pitcher's. Thus, he was actually pounding the ball into his own glove. The pitcher, realizing what was going on, would get off the mound to comply with a rule concerning this trick play. Moments later, another out would be recorded.

Travis Fryman said the trick works because "most players aren't good base runners." He said that if a runner is alert and doesn't stray off a base when the pitcher isn't on the mound, he simply can't get suckered by the hidden ball play. Like many experts, Fryman also feels that Spike Owen was one of the great players at pulling off this trick.

Screen Play

Some tricky third basemen run their own version of a screen play when a runner is at third in a sacrifice-fly situation. Knowing the runner must wait until he sees the outfielder snag the ball before he can tag up, a wily third baseman might purposely get his body in such a position as to block the view of the runner. If the runner can't see the exact moment of the catch, he'll be a second or so slower at leaving the base and, thus, a step or two slower reaching home.

Red Hot Chili

In 1995, Sandy Alomar's backup catcher, Tony Peña, and Dennis Martinez recreated one of the most famous trick plays ever. The first time this bit of deception took place was during the 1972 World Series. The Oakland A's were in a situation in which an intentional walk to Johnny Bench made sense. They went through the motions, but at the last second they fired strike three past the befuddled Bench.

Actually, World Series–bound Cleveland did the A's one better

—they got away with it on two occasions. Peña and Martinez cooked up the play on their own. Alomar recalled: "Dennis was struggling, and he needed a play to get out of an inning. He had thrown a lot of pitches, and it was a perfect situation to do it. It was a smart play. It worked on Chili Davis who was very upset about it. They did it one time to John Olerud."

It seems incredible that this play could work twice in a season in this day and age when highlights are constantly played and replayed on television. Alomar concurred, "If I'm a player for a different team, I guarantee you I see that on ESPN, and they wouldn't get me."

Jeter Approves

The 1996 American League Rookie of the Year, Derek Jeter, was asked what trick plays he's seen that were interesting or unusual. Without skipping a beat, the Yankee shortstop responded, "Tony LaRussa batting the pitcher eighth over there in St. Louis—that's a little different!"

Arguments aside about whether or not this is actually a trick play, he's right. On July 9, 1998, when he penciled his starter in at the number-eight spot, LaRussa made Todd Stottlemyre the first big league pitcher in twenty years to bat anywhere but last in the order. Although Stottlemyre did hit .236 the previous season, there was another reason for the strategy. At first, some fans thought LaRussa was doing this because the man who did bat ninth, Placido Polanco, might be a weak hitter. Also, Polanco was making just his second major league start.

Fans and writers recalled that the last pitcher to hit higher than ninth was Philadelphia's Steve Carlton on June 1, 1979. In that case, it was true that Carlton was often a bigger threat with the bat than, say, Bud Harrelson, who hit ninth when Carlton was in the number-eight spot.

After much speculation, the truth came out. LaRussa revealed that his motive for the move was to get more men on base ahead of the heart of the lineup. Not a bad thought, especially when the aorta of that heart is big Mark McGwire, who was in the midst of chasing Roger Maris and the single-season home run record of 61.

Said the St. Louis manager, "I don't see how it doesn't make sense for the ninth-place hitter to be a legitimate hitter. This gives us a better shot to score runs. It's an extra guy on base in front of Ray Lankford, Mark McGwire, and Brian Jordan. The more guys who are on base, the less they'll be able to pitch around Mark."

LaRussa said he first conceived of the scheme at the All-Star break and that it "doesn't have anything to do with the pitcher." Nothing, that is, except get his weak bat out of the way and allow a real hitter in the ninth spot to become, in effect, an additional leadoff hitter in front of McGwire and Company.

A logical question for LaRussa, then, was why not just drop McGwire to the cleanup position so he could always have three bona fide hitters preceding him. However, LaRussa said that because McGwire hits third, he comes to the plate in the 1st inning of every game, a big advantage in LaRussa's book.

Lame Trick

Many baseball fans feel the trick play in which the pitcher fakes a throw towards the runner off third base, then swivels, fires, and tries to pick off the runner from first is lame. Somehow, though, it succeeded in 1998.

On the last day in June, the Oakland A's were hosting the San Diego Padres. Entering the top of the ninth, Oakland was clinging to a 12–8 lead. Two outs later, the Padres were rallying. They had scored two runs. Now they had a runner at third with the tying run on first.

With a 2-and-2 count on Mark Sweeney, A's catcher Mike Macfarlane gave reliever Mike Fetters the sign to put on a special pickoff move. Fetters, however, was confused—he had spent the last six years with the Milwaukee Brewers and momentarily mixed up their signals with those of the A's.

So Macfarlane waved his hand in the direction of first, then third to indicate what he wanted. Even after all of that blatant gesturing, Padres runner Ruben Rivera was caught snoozing. Eventually, the rookie Rivera was tagged out trying to make it to second base.

A's manager Art Howe was thinking along the lines of Tony Peña when he called his trick play. "It just didn't seem like anybody was going to make an out, so I said, 'Let's manufacture one,'" commented Howe.

The play was especially mortifying for several reasons. For example, it's foolish to do anything risky (or not pay attention) on the bases in such a situation. After all, this play ended the game and gave the A's a win. Not only that, Rivera was in the game for his running skills—the Padres had just put him in moments earlier as a pinch runner.

Oakland's Jason Giambi observed, "You know the old theory about that play never working? Well, it did today."

Chapter Five

WHO SAID IT?

Baseball has always produced colorful, funny, and interesting quotes. Some of these lines have worked their way into everyday lingo, and some have even become a part of Americana. Who can forget such bits of wisdom as Satchel Paige's "Don't look back. Something might be gaining on you"?

Now it's your turn to read a quote and to match it up with the person who uttered it. So, get started. (Match-up answers are given at the end of the chapter.)

Match-up: Managers' Words

1. Who said, in discussing his team's home park: "When you come to the plate in this ballpark, you're in scoring position"?

2. Who made the egotistical comment "Stay close in the early innings, and I'll think of something"?

3. What diminutive skipper said these fiery words: "I think there should be bad blood between all teams"?

4. What manager, saddled with an inept team, moaned, "Can't anyone here play this game?"

5. Who said, "You don't save a pitcher for tomorrow. Tomorrow it may rain"? Big clue: He's also famous for saying, "Nice guys finish last"—although that wasn't exactly what he said.

6. After suffering through a tough road trip, what Reds manager of 1997 said, "When it rains it pours, and we're in the midst of a monsoon"?

a. Charlie Dressen
b. Don Baylor
c. Earl Weaver
d. Casey Stengel
e. Ray Knight
f. Leo Durocher

Match-up: Humor

1. When told his salary was more than the earnings of President Hoover, this man stated, "Oh, yeah? Well, I had a better year than he had."

2. On his disdain for artificial grass, this slugger commented, "If a horse can't eat it, I don't want to play on it."

3. When asked for the highlight of his career, this player responded, "I walked with the bases loaded to drive in the winning run in an intrasquad game in spring training."

4. Although he probably wasn't trying to be humorous, this good ol' country boy once said, "They X-rayed my head and didn't find anything."

5. Speaking of his dislike for hitting in Comiskey Park, this player said, "At Wrigley Field, I feel like King Kong. Here, I feel like Donkey Kong."

a. Gary Gaetti
b. Bob Uecker
c. Babe Ruth
d. Dick Allen
e. Dizzy Dean

Match-up: More Managers

1. Even though he'd won a World Series in the 1990s, this manager once muttered, "I'm not sure whether I'd rather be managing or testing bulletproof vests."

2. This man's team was injury plagued in 1989, prompting him to observe, "If World War III broke out, I'd guarantee you we'd win the pennant by 20 games. All our guys would be 4-F. They couldn't pass the physical."

3. In 1997, this White Sox skipper philosophized, "I learned a long time ago, in this game you might as well take the blame because you're going to get it anyway."

4. His pitcher entered the game with the bases loaded. Two wild pitches later, the bases were empty because all three men had scored, leading to this managerial quip: "Well, that's one way to pitch out of a bases-loaded jam." Clue: He was managing the Brewers when this occurred.

    a. Terry Bevington   c. Whitey Herzog
    b. Tom Trebelhorn   d. Joe Torre

Match-up: Last Call for Managers' Quotes

1. Lucky enough to be the manager of George Brett, this man was asked what he told Brett regarding hitting. The Royals manager replied, "I tell him, 'Attaway to hit, George.'"

2. Never known for his use of grammar, this great manager once said of a player's injury, "There's nothing wrong with his shoulder except some pain, and pain don't hurt you."

3. On what it takes to be a successful manager, an all-time big-name manager opined, "A sense of humor and a good bullpen."

4. Two quotes from the same man. A) "I'm not the manager because I'm always right, but I'm always right because I'm the manager." B) "The worst thing about managing is the day you realize you want to win more than your players do."

5. This manager-for-one-day naively believed, "Managing isn't all that difficult. Just score more runs than the other guy."

    a. Ted Turner   d. Jim Frey
    b. Whitey Herzog   e. Sparky Anderson
    c. Gene Mauch

Match-up: This and That

1. Who said: "Baseball statistics are a lot like a girl in a bikini. They show a lot, but not everything"?

2. Two quotes from an ex-catcher: A) "When Steve [Carlton] and I die, we are going to be buried 60 feet, 6 inches apart." B) On Bob Gibson: "He is the luckiest pitcher I ever saw. He always pitched when the other team didn't score any runs."

3. During 1998 spring training, this man came to camp overweight. He joked, "I must have had five coaches come up to me and say, 'I expected to see you floating over the stadium tied to a string...'"

4. Who was so arrogant that he once proclaimed, "The only reason I don't like playing in the World Series is I can't watch myself play"?

5. Soon after being traded, a disgruntled player, asked about the condition of his shoulder, replied, "My shoulder's O.K., but I've still got a scar where the Mets stuck the knife in my back."

a. Dante Bichette
b. Toby Harrah
c. Tug McGraw

d. Tim McCarver
e. Reggie Jackson

Match-up: More This and That

1. This manager summarized the futures of two 20-year-old prospects, saying, "In ten years, Ed Kranepool has a chance to be a star. In ten years, Greg Goosen has a chance to be thirty."

2. This Hall-of-Famer said, "So what if I'm ugly? I never saw anyone hit with his face."

3. Tired of being reduced to sitting on the bench, and ignoring his lack of productivity, this man said his team was guilty of the "worst betrayal by a team in all sports history. It's not fair to Deion Sanders. It's not fair to teammates or to the fans,

either. It's one of the worst things ever done to a player."
P.S.: His team went on to win the World Series without him.

4. After fanning in a two-out, potential game-winning situation in the bottom of the 9th inning, this Pittsburgh Pirate of the past lamented, "It's what you dream of right there...either you're Billy the Kid or Billy the Goat."

a. Glenn Wilson	c. Deion Sanders
b. Casey Stengel	d. Yogi Berra

Match-up: More Humor

1. Who said: "I've never played with a pitcher who tried to hit a batter in the head. Most pitchers are like me. If I'm going to hit somebody, I'm going to aim for the bigger parts"?

2. This West Virginia native wasn't too worldly when he broke into the majors. During his ride to Wrigley Field for his first visit there, he spotted Lake Michigan and asked, "What ocean is that?"

3. Who was the player Dante Bichette was referring to when he said: "He's the kid who, when he played Little League, all the parents called the president of the league and said, 'Get him out of there, I don't want him to hurt my son.' I had my mom call the National League office to see if she could do for me"?

4. What player was former pitcher Darold Knowles talking about when he uttered these words: "There isn't enough mustard in the world to cover him"?

5. Who said: "We live by the Golden Rule—those who have the gold make the rules"?

a. Bert Blyleven	d. Mark McGwire
b. Buzzi Bavasi	e. Reggie Jackson
c. John Kruk	

Match-up: Colorful Quotes

1. What American League pitcher said of his first trip to Yankee Stadium, "The first time I ever came into a game there, I got in the bullpen car, and they told me to lock the doors"?

2. This pitcher apparently got tired of being asked trite questions from reporters. Once, after surrendering a home run that cost him a 1–0 defeat, he was asked what it was he had thrown to game hero Tony Conigliaro. The succinct reply was, "It was a baseball."

3. This manager did so well, he was rewarded by the Cardinals. Owner August Busch, who was eighty-five at the time, told the manager he could have a lifetime contract. The St. Louis skipper countered with, "Whose lifetime? Yours or mine?"

4. This colorful character was a fine pitcher. His World Series ledger was golden: 6–0 with a 2.86 ERA. When asked to explain his success, he attributed it to "clean living and a fast outfield."

a. Joe Horlen
b. Mike Flannagan

c. Lefty Gomez
d. Whitey Herzog

Match-up: Final Inning

1. This peppery manager would upstage umpires at the drop of a hat. He even loved to peck umps with the beak of his hat. He offered one of his most famous lines after he showed up the umpires by taking a rule book out on the field. He stated, "There ain't no rule in the rule book about bringing a rule book on the field."

2. This umpire had a rivalry with the manager from the above quote. He once said, "That midget can barely see over the top of the dugout steps, and he claims he can see the pitches."

3. An ex-pitcher, this announcer butchered the English language. In one case, he said a player had "slud into third" instead of "slid." Another remark was, "Don't fail to miss tomorrow's game."

4. After hitting four homers in a game to tie the single-game record, this power hitter said quite correctly, "I had a good week today."

a. Earl Weaver   c. Dizzy Dean
b. Marty Springstead   d. Bob Horner

ANSWERS
"Who Said It?" Match-ups

Managers' Words	Last Call for Managers' Quotes	More Humor
1. b	1. d	1. a
2. a	2. e	2. c
3. c	3. b	3. d
4. d	4. c	4. e
5. f	5. a	5. b
6. e		

Humor	This and That	Colorful Quotes
1. c	1. b	1. b
2. d	2. d	2. a
3. b	3. a	3. d
4. e	4. e	4. c
5. a	5. c	

More Managers	More This and That	Final Inning
1. d	1. b	1. a
2. c	2. d	2. b
3. a	3. c	3. c
4. b	4. a	4. d

Chapter Six

HAS IT EVER HAPPENED?

There are things that have happened in baseball that are incredibly hard to believe. Just imagine: Chicago Cubs outfielder Hack Wilson once actually drove home 191 runs during a single season, and he did it in a mere 155 games. This chapter tests your knowledge of similarly improbable events.

To keep you honest, every once in a while we'll throw you a wicked curveball, such as a trick question. Then, we'll try to fool you with a change-up in which one of the "facts" in the question will be off by a gnat's eyelash. Your job is to determine the truth and figure out if our events ever really happened.

Potent Lineup

Has a team ever had as many as six players in the lineup drive in 100 or more runs during a season?

Answer: No, but the 1936 Yankees featured an incredibly productive lineup with a record five men who had more than 100 ribbies.

The men included three future Hall-of-Famers: first baseman Lou Gehrig, who amassed 152 RBI; center fielder Joe DiMaggio, who added 125; and catcher Bill Dickey with his 107 RBI. In addition, Tony Lazzeri had 109, and George Selkirk contributed 107.

No-Hit Glory

Has a pitcher ever come up with a no-hitter during his very first start?

Amazingly, the answer is yes. More amazingly, the pitcher wasn't very good at all. Alva "Bobo" Holloman had pitched exclusively out of the bullpen. Then, after begging owner Bill Veeck to give him a start, he came up with his gem back in 1953. Although Holloman succeeded that day, his luck didn't last; he was gone from the majors for good just a short time later that same year.

His career statistics are paltry: 3 wins versus 7 losses, an ERA of 5.23, and twice as many walks (50) as batters struck out. His no-hitter was his only complete game ever.

The 300 Club

Certain numbers have a magical quality in baseball. For example, as a rule, if a hitter connects for 500 homers, he's headed for the Hall of Fame. For pitchers, making it into the 300-Win Club—a highly exclusive circle of stars—is a coveted goal. Has a pitcher ever managed to lose 300 games?

Answer: Yes, and ironically the man to lose the most games in big league history (313 to be precise) is the same man whose name graces the trophy that personifies pitching excellence—Cy Young. So the award given for pitching excellence actually has its origin with the game's biggest loser. Of course, to be fair, Young also won a staggering 511 games, the most ever in the annals of the game. The next highest win total is nearly 100 less than that—Walter Johnson's 416 victories.

By the way, the only other man to drop 300 decisions was an obscure pitcher from the late nineteenth century named Pud Galvin. This right-hander made it to the Hall of Fame, as did Young. Galvin pitched only 14 years, yet he won 361 games and had such unusual numbers as a 46–29 won–lost record in 1883 and 46–22 the next season. Imagine, he won 92 games in just two years—that's four and a half to five years' worth of toil for a good pitcher today. Of course, his 51 losses over that two-year span would also take quite a few years for a good pitcher to reach today.

27-Game Winner with a Loser?

Has a team that finished in last place ever produced a 27-game winning pitcher? Could a lousy team score enough runs and support a pitcher well enough for him to have a chance to win 27 games?

Answer: This has happened once. Steve Carlton, one of the greatest lefties ever, pitched for the hapless Philadelphia Phillies of 1972 and accomplished just that. The Phils finished sixth in the six-team National League East Division that year with a 59–97 record (.378 won–loss percentage). They were so far behind first-place Pittsburgh that they needed a spyglass and a crow's nest to see the Pirates.

Despite that, Carlton went 27–10, good for an astronomical .730 won–loss percentage. He accounted for nearly half the Phillies wins that year (45.8 percent to be exact). His ERA was a minuscule 1.97 over a workhorse 346$^{1/3}$ innings. That's not all. He also fanned 310 men while walking only 87. He even chalked up 30 complete games in registering one of the most dominant years ever. His reward was a unanimous Cy Young Award, making him the only pitcher from a last-place team to ever earn that trophy.

Fanning Infrequently

Has a major-leaguer gone an entire season while striking out fewer than, say, 25 times?

Answer: Not in a long time, but yes, it has been done. In fact, Cleveland's Joe Sewell did this with ease. Sewell was known for his bat control, and, in 1925 and 1929, he truly showcased that talent. During those seasons, he struck out a mere eight times, four each year. Men have been known to strike out four times in a day; it took an entire year for Sewell to do that. Furthermore, he had 608 at bats in 1925 and 578 in 1929.

Switch Pitcher?

Has a modern-day pitcher ever thrown with both arms during a major league game?

Answer: Yes, and it happened in the not-too-distant past. As the 1995 season came to an end, Greg Harris, a Montreal Expo right-handed pitcher (also listed as a switch hitter), faced the Cincinnati Reds. He threw a scoreless 9th inning while pitching with both arms. Naturally he threw left-handed to lefty batters and right-handed to righties.

Prior to Harris, one player, with the poetic name of Ed Head, also used both arms in an inning. He did so because he had injured the arm he normally used.

World Series Excellence

Was there ever a World Series in which every game was decided by a shutout?

Answer: Indeed there was. During the dead-ball era, specifically in 1905, the New York Giants won the Series in five contests. They did it mainly by riding their ace pitcher, Christy Mathewson. He won games one, three, and the finale by scores of 3–0, 9–0, and 2–0, as he fired 27 straight shutout innings.

The other Giants win belonged to Joe McGinnity, known as "Iron Man," who produced a 1–0 beauty in the fourth game. McGinnity even pitched well in the only loss to the Philadelphia Athletics, a shutout fired by Chief Bender. As a matter of fact, only three men pitched for New York in that Series, and the third man did so for just 1 inning. Their combined ERA for the Series was invisible at 0.00! Philadelphia scored just three runs in all.

Better Than Perfect

This question involves a very famous game that took place in the 1950s. Did a pitcher ever throw a perfect game that went beyond 9 innings?

Answer: Even though the above question seems to give away the answer, this question, like a Gaylord Perry pitch, is loaded. While it's true Harvey Haddix threw a perfect game that went into the 13th inning back in 1959, a bizarre ruling by baseball officials in 1991 took away his perfect game status. The rule states that in order for a pitcher to get credit for a no-hitter, he must pitch at least 9 innings and pitch a complete game without surrendering a hit. Therefore, what most experts agree was the most perfect game ever is not recognized as such.

Here's what happened on that historic night. Haddix, a di-minutive lefty for the Pirates, was perfect through 12 innings against the Milwaukee Braves. Felix Mantilla led off the 13th and reached base on a throwing error by Pirates third base-man Don Hoak. Eddie Mathews then sacrificed the runner to scoring position. That prompted Pittsburgh manager Danny Murtaugh to issue an intentional walk to the dangerous Hank Aaron, setting up a double play.

Pandemonium ensued when Joe Adcock homered. But, due to yet another baseball rule, he only received credit for a double. The reason he was robbed of a home run isn't quite as bizarre

as the ruling that hurt Haddix, however. Aaron saw the ball soaring deep and figured it would drop near the fence, so he touched second base, but he never bothered to go to third. As Adcock rounded the bags and touched third base, he was technically guilty of passing a runner and, therefore, received credit for two bases, not four. Adcock also received just one run batted-in instead of three.

Martinez Also Robbed

In 1995, Montreal Expos pitcher Pedro Martinez also got ripped off by the new no-hitter rule. Facing the Padres, he was perfect through 9 innings. Shortly thereafter, when Bip Roberts doubled to lead off the tenth, the perfect game was gone. Martinez then gave way to closer Mel Rojas, who retired the last three batters. The Expos went on to win a 1–0 classic.

Impotent Bats

Has there ever been a season in which nobody in the entire American League hit .300 or better? Could such a season of pitchers' domination occur?

Answer: Although there was never a season without at least one .300 hitter, there was a year in which only one man topped that level. The year 1968 was known as the "Year of the Pitcher." That season, the American League batting title went to Boston's Carl Yastrzemski, who hit .301. The next-best average was a paltry .290. The A.L. pitchers prevailed that year; five of them had ERAs under 2.00.

That was also the season that one of every 5 games resulted in a shutout. It seemed as if every time St. Louis Cardinal Bob Gibson pitched, he tossed a shutout (he had 13). His ERA (1.12) was the fourth lowest in baseball history. Finally, that season also featured the game's last 30-game winner, Detroit's Denny McLain (31–6).

Chapter Seven

THE LIFE OF ROOKIES

There's an old story, probably more baseball lore than truth, that sums up just how gullible rookies can be. It goes like this:

A rookie was on the mound in a tense situation. After surrendering a key hit, he was lifted from the game. The manager asked him what pitch he had just thrown. The rookie replied it was a fastball, but a poor one because he had lost his grip on the ball. He told his manager his hands were too sweaty to get a good hold on the baseball. "Why didn't you use the rosin bag?" the manager asked. According to the story, the pitcher replied, "Because I couldn't get it open."

While we won't swear to the validity of that story, it's true that the life of a rookie is never easy. From being subjected to cruel tricks to being forced to sing songs in front of the team (usually humiliatingly off key), newcomers go through quite a bit. As you read these true tales of rookies, use your imagination to envision what the life of a big league rookie is like.

Boggs Speaks

Wade Boggs of Tampa Bay offered an explanation of the change in the treatment rookies receive today. Concerning their reaction to being treated like peons, Boggs said, "It's probably less tolerated by rookies now. They get a little bit more offensive more often [nowadays]. I don't know when the transition period [to that attitude] happened, probably in 1991 and 1992.

"Rookies get to the big leagues and sort of have an attitude that they've been here ten years. When I came up [in 1982 at the age of 24] with [Carl] Yastrzemski, [Mike] Torrez, [Dennis] Eckersley, [Jerry] Remy, and that type of individual [established veterans], it was a lot different.

"Rookies are to been seen and not heard," the six-time batting champ continued. "You keep your mouth shut. You learn your business, go about it, and put your time in. I think that's a lost art of paying your dues and keeping your mouth shut.

"I'm sure their money [big contracts now] has changed their attitude," he stated. He suggested that because Tampa Bay was an expansion club, things were a bit different. With so many young players, it's almost as if the whole team is made of rookies. In fact, sixteen of the forty players on their start-of-the-season roster were listed as first-year players. Boggs could report, then, that "The kids around here are very hard workers, willing to learn and have respect for the veterans."

Long Ago

From Boggs and his overview of the way things were and how they are now, let's flash back to long ago. In the old days, a rookie would not only get hazed, be the target of pranks and be tormented by teammates, he might even encounter treasonous behavior.

There's a story of a veteran catcher from the early days of baseball who had little regard for upstart, rookie hurlers. They say that the catcher, in situations which weren't crucial (such as two outs and nobody aboard), would actually tip off opposing batters as to what pitch was coming. He'd call for, say, a fastball, and then he'd whisper to the batter that a juicy fastball was coming down the pipe. It would have been tough enough for a hurler facing a veteran batter without him knowing what's coming, but that was the plight of some rookies way back when.

More on the Good Ol' Days

Long ago, veterans would nail a rookie's spikes to the clubhouse floor. This trick not only wouldn't be played today, it couldn't be done because of the plush carpeting in most clubhouses.

Giving a rookie (or any teammate, for that matter) a hot foot was popular back in the days of the dead ball.

Ray Miller chipped in with the times veterans would "nail their shoes to their locker, juvenile stuff." It may be puerile, but that's the nature of such ribbing.

Even Pittsburgh Hall of Fame shortstop Honus Wagner was chased out of the batting cage by veterans. Other greats such as Babe Ruth and Lou Gehrig got similar treatment. Ruth would go to the bat rack for a favorite bat only to discover the handle had been sawed off. Gehrig's bats were once sawed into four parts. On one occasion, Joe Bush, a teammate, called Gehrig "a stupid college punk," and there was no teasing in that voice. Carl Mays was also particularly cruel to Gehrig.

One reason veterans in baseball's early days were so abusive was that they were afraid youngsters would come along and take their jobs or the jobs of their friends.

Life on the Trains

Players of that era traveled long distances by train. Rookies were routinely assigned the worst sleeping quarters, upper berths on the last of the sleeper cars. Those were the cars that were the most unstable as they whipped around curves. After all, if anyone was going to get a bad case of *mal de mer* on land, it would be the lowly rooks.

Veterans would sometimes pull this one on rookies: The player chosen to be the "mark" would be told that there was a shoe thief on board the train. This opening gambit was credible back then, since players would leave their shoes on the floor outside their sleeping quarters when they went to bed. A porter would come along during the night and take the shoes away to have them polished. The rookie, though, didn't know about the shoeshine service, so he'd believe the tale of the mysterious thief.

The rookie was then told he'd have to stand guard and grab any suspicious characters lurking about. Sure enough, when the porter picked up a pair of shoes, the diligent rookie would grab the "culprit" while shouting excitedly about his great detective work. His reward was a chorus of laughter.

Phenom Number One

David Clyde broke into the majors in 1973 with the Texas Rangers, accompanied by Texas-sized hype. The ink was still wet on this 18-year-old's high school diploma when he made his big league debut. The fans' initial reaction to Clyde was not unlike what would happen three years later in Detroit with Mark "The Bird" Fidrych. Attendance boomed for the last-place Rangers, and the front office was understandably happy. (At least for the time being—Clyde went 4–8 and never really panned out.)

Despite all this, Clyde was treated with contempt by veterans. One teammate said, "Don't think I'm going to be your friend, because you're out after my job." And those were the first words immediately after the two players met!

Phenom Number Two

Wilson Alvarez also had an interesting start to his career. He threw a no-hitter in his first start with the White Sox. Despite such glory, he was treated like a typical rookie. "I always was the last guy to get to do things [such as hit in the batting cage]," Alvarez said. "It was, 'Get out of the way. Let me do my job first, and you do it after.' But I understood that. The guys who had been in the league for a long time need to work, and we'd respect that."

More Train (and Boat) Tales

Rookies weren't experienced in the ways of the world in the early days. One player, traveling by boat from New York to Boston, was conned into sleeping (very fitfully) in a life preserver.

Then there's the famous story of Babe Ruth's first train ride. He was on a train headed from Baltimore to Fayetteville as a member of the Orioles. The veterans looked upon him as a naive and overgrown child, so they gave him the then-common nickname "Babe." (Other "naming" stories exist, including one connected with Ed Barrow.) They made sure that Ruth spent his first night in an embarrassing posture.

Next to each Pullman upper berth was a sort of small hammock for players to place their clothes in. However, veteran Ben Egan told Ruth that its real purpose was for pitchers to rest their throwing arms. Ruth said the hammock held his arm in an uncomfortable position all night and that he went sleepless as a result. But, he figured, if that's what a big leaguer does, then so be it.

The result was humiliation and a very stiff arm the next day. Ruth called it "the first Oriole injury of 1914." He later said he had fallen for the oldest gag in baseball.

Dick Williams, the only manager to guide three different teams to the World Series, summed it up, "If you go way back, it was very tough on a first-year man. Now it's more business-like. The money is better, but they have less fun now."

Practical Jokes

Williams recalled another practical joke. He continued, "Someone would leave a message in the player's box telling him to report early for extra hitting the next day." Of course, the duped youngster would show up, but he'd be all alone.

Jay Johnstone, a legendary prankster, who roamed outfields from 1966 to 1985, used a similar joke. He'd send an official-looking letter to a raw rookie instructing him to appear at, say, a local television station for an interview. The rookie would beam with self-satisfaction until later, when he realized he'd been had.

The Red Baron Strikes Again

Rick "The Red Baron" Sutcliffe not only won a Cy Young trophy, he deserved the title "Prince of Pranks" as well. As a member of the Cubs in 1991, Sutcliffe was in the dugout when catcher Erik Pappas gathered his first big league hit. Sutcliffe retrieved the ball that had been underhanded into the dugout for safekeeping.

Realizing Pappas would want to preserve the souvenir of the proud moment, Sutcliffe's devilish mind began to churn. He inscribed the date and Pappas's name on the ball. Then, when Pappas trotted into the dugout, the pitcher presented him with the prized trophy. However, according to Pappas, "He used an old ball instead of the real game ball from my first hit. He purposely spelled my name wrong." Pappas naturally thought Sutcliffe had defaced the ball for a gag. At least that was a mild trick and one that was easily rectified.

In 1998, the Indians played a similar joke on rookie Alex Ramirez. After banging out his first hit, the veterans gave him a fake souvenir ball that was muddy and grass-stained. Once they got the reaction they wanted, they told him the truth and gave him the bona fide ball.

Rookie Batboys

Even a rookie batboy won't escape tricks. Indians manager Mike Hargrove told the story of how Sutcliffe would send a batboy looking for the key to the batter's box. Everybody was in on the joke, and they'd send the kid on a sort of wild scavenger hunt from clubhouse to clubhouse. "Sometimes," said the manager, who won the A.L. pennant in 1995 and 1997, "we'd send a guy for a bag of knuckleballs or curveballs."

Did they truly fall for such stunts? "Sometimes," responded Hargrove with a smile. "It never hurt to try."

Lasorda/LaRussa Tag Team

In 1992, Oakland A's manager Tony LaRussa borrowed a favorite gag from Tommy Lasorda. Kirk Dressendorfer's spring-training performance had earned him the fifth spot in the pitching rotation. Yet on April 1, the day of LaRussa's conniving, the rookie pitcher wasn't aware he had made the team. Not only that, he probably didn't have much confidence going into camp, because players who were assigned jersey numbers such as his 60 don't usually head up north with the big boys who make the 25-man roster.

Therefore, when LaRussa told Dressendorfer he had been cut from the team, the pitcher sadly jogged off the diamond. LaRussa later said, "It was an April Fools' joke. He went to clean out his locker. Dave Duncan [pitching coach] called him over to say good-bye." It was only then, after all the theatrics, that Dressendorfer heard some laughter and realized it was all a joke.

"It had me a little worried," he admitted. "Then I saw them laughing. I thought it was pretty cold." He's correct, of course. Humor at the expense of rookies has always been rather ruthless.

Poor House Humor

Back in 1975, pitcher Fritz Peterson kept things loose in the Indians' spring-training locker room. A teammate of his, Duane Kuiper, looked back on a favorite trick. "Cy Buynak [the clubhouse attendant] would leave the weekly bill for clubhouse dues, say for $30, on players' chairs," said Kuiper. "Fritz put a '1' in front of the '30' on the rookies' bills. They'd see it [as a bill for $130] and almost die! They didn't know anything, and they'd believe everything."

Physical Humor

Players today still execute the classic "three-man lift." Cleveland slugger Jim Thome explained how the Indians did it in 1994. "The older guys tricked [rookies] Manny Ramirez and Julian Tavares into laying down for the 'lift.' One of the guys said to Manny and Julian, 'I bet I can lift you two up,'" said Thome.

At that stage, the two players went along with it, getting down on the floor, one on either side of the veteran, who was bragging of his strongman prowess. Thome continued, "The three guys interlock hands, and usually the middle guy is the one who knows what's going on. So, when he's interlocked, the other two guys are trapped. That's when everybody comes up and lifts their shirts over their heads and puts baby powder and shaving cream on them. They even dumped trash on them. They can't go anywhere. That was the funniest thing I ever saw in baseball."

Variation on the Three-Man Theme

Fred Patek said players in his era, the 1960s and even earlier, loved the trick Thome described. Patek remembered, "They [his Pirate teammates] almost got me twice." The first time, they got him using the conventional means. Then, the second time, "They said it had something to do with stretching. The equipment manager set it up. They told me Steve Blass was going to be the victim, but I saw him with some aftershave lotion, shaving cream, and Tuff Skin. That's when I caught on and took off."

Incidentally, some teams used worse torture ingredients than the Pirates did. Some spread nasty-smelling liniments or blistering-hot ointments all over first-year players.

Traditional Trick

In 1997, Pittsburgh rookies Jose Guillen and Jeff Granger were flabbergasted when two Chicago policemen entered the Pirates clubhouse at Wrigley Field. When the officers told the two players that they were under arrest, they became apoplectic. The policemen announced that Guillen and Granger were being charged with vandalism.

It seems they went along with a National League ritual requiring rookies to vandalize a famous Chicago statue of a general on horseback. The tradition involves painting the private parts of the horse using the rookies' team colors. Later Guillen would claim he knew it was all a gag. He also confessed he was guilty of going along with the ritual saying, "Every rookie has to do it."

As the prank continued, Granger actually asked if he could

make his one phone call. Only then did they tell the partners-in-crime that it was all a joke.

From Vandalism to Grand Theft Auto

Shane Monahan broke into the majors with the Seattle Mariners. During 1998, his rookie season, his veteran teammates played a unique prank on the outfielder. It seems the Mariners were staging a promotion called "Turn Ahead the Clock" as a variation on the nostalgic "Turn Back the Clock" day that many teams run.

Between innings, the Mariners gave prizes away to the fans. At one point, Seattle veterans arranged to have Monahan's 1996 Ford Explorer taken from the players' parking area and driven around the field. The public address announcer said they were giving the Explorer away and read the seat number of the winning fan.

The veterans went so far as to include the "winner" in on the trick. The "fan" began to leap up and down in excitement while Monahan began to panic. Finally, he spied a chuckling Ken Griffey, Jr., on the bench and the realization hit him—he had been had!

Orosco Speaks

Jesse Orosco broke into the majors in 1979, so he's seen it all. He commented, "Now when tricks happen, you would think the kids would've heard about them growing up, but they still get caught with them. Evidently, somebody's not really passing history on. We're probably glad that they don't. This way we can keep getting the rookies, so it's kinda fun.

"I remember the mongoose trick they did in Cincinnati for a lot of years. You can do it tomorrow to somebody before batting practice, and I guarantee you you're gonna get somebody who hasn't heard about it growing up." The trick he alluded to starts by telling a rookie that there's a wild mongoose trapped inside a box in the clubhouse. Warily, the rube will approach the box and, as he gets close, a veteran releases the "mongoose" using a spring mechanism. A hairy-looking fake creature seems to bolt out of the box directly at the victim, who invariably recoils in fear.

Cross-Dressing

The treatment a rookie gets can depend upon his status. For example, Dwight Gooden was a big name by the time he made it to the majors with the New York Mets. He stated, "I was lucky, actually. They were pretty good with me." On the other hand, he related that when Ryan Thompson came over to the Mets in a trade for David Cone, "We made him wear a dress in Philadelphia because he's from that area. His family was there, and we hid his clothes so he had to wear a dress and high-heel shoes on the bus."

Getting back to Alvarez, he had similar recollections. "The

rookies were dressed in funny outfits, sometimes like a woman. They'd make them do that in New York and go out and sign autographs for the fans looking like that. Or they'd make them dress like that and have them walk through a mall," Alvarez remembered.

Pitcher Pete Harnisch went into more detail on the type of clothes rookies had to wear, citing, "wacky shoes, outdated, old-fashioned ones like platform shoes and bad suits—purple, whatever."

Pat Corrales said that things are similar in Atlanta, but he tacked on a few items to Harnisch's list: "Our rookies here have to wear an outfit, and they get some loud, ugly, late-'60s outfits—lime, purple, bell bottoms, big lapel [shirts], ugly polyester stuff, and big thick platform shoes." The Braves, he said, make the rookies wear these outlandish clothes on their first road trip.

However, when Corrales broke in, there was no such levity. He echoed the words of Boggs: "You kinda had to keep your mouth shut and do what you were told."

Meanwhile, Tampa Bay's Quinton McCracken tossed in a few more sartorial notes, "There's always the patented dressing them up in tutus and sitting in front of the plane [like that]. As a rookie, I took it in stride. It's a fun part of the game. It's part of the tradition of baseball."

Still More Sartorial Items

The 1995 Indians went a slightly different route when they got rookie Herbert Perry. Shortly after the last game of his first road trip to Toronto, he was about to get dressed when he noticed, "All of my clothes were missing from my locker. I had to wear these hobo clothes [thoughtfully provided by veterans] all the way back through the airport. I swear, I thought there was no way they [American customs officials] were going to let me back into the country."

During a 1998 interview, Rafael Palmeiro said, "Earlier this year, we played the Marlins, and they have a bunch of young guys, rookies. Their clubhouse was on the other side [of the field from their dugout], so they have to come through a tunnel, come through where we come out of our clubhouse doors. It was the funniest thing—there were 12 babies with nothing on but big diapers. It was half their team with these diapers." It was bad enough for them to have to parade around their own locker room dressed in that style, but to have to be on display for the opponents was unbelievable.

Of course, Chicago White Sox rookies probably think they have it even worse. The tradition there is to have Robin Ventura pick out superhero costumes for the first-year players to wear on chartered flights.

St. Louis Blues

Chris Chambliss also recalled typical tricks on rookies: "In St. Louis there was a tradition where they take the rookies and make them dress in different [wild and weird] clothes on road trips. One time, we did it after we lost a game, and that didn't go over too good, but not much of that happens anymore."

Alvarez agrees with Chambliss that the treatment of rookies has changed. "It's not like when I broke in," he said. "The last couple of years, it's changed a lot. Most of the guys are treated the same—like everybody else."

Yankee Point of View

Most of today's players and observers believe that not only are tricks on rookies milder than in the old days, but they also occur less frequently. Scott Brosius of the 1998 Yankees said, "Especially this team here, they don't do a lot of things like that. I've never seen anything out of the ordinary [here].

"I think the game's a little bit different now. The money that they make now is so much different, so some of those traditions have started to fade away," said Chambliss.

He added that at times a rookie's ordeal was to serve the veterans when a group of players went out to eat. Now, he says, even eating out with a bunch of players is dying out. Players aren't together as much as they used to be, so "some of those pranks don't really exist anymore."

Chambliss also pointed out that in the old days, "the older guys got more swings [in the batting cage] than the rookies, but nowadays everybody gets the same amount of swings because batting practice is so structured."

While Chambliss may be correct that rookies aren't treated badly anymore, that line of thinking isn't new. As long ago as 1945, Ty Cobb said veterans gave him a hard time when newspapers started giving him a lot of publicity in his rookie year. Veterans hazed him because they were jealous. Cobb stated that every time he'd leave his hat unguarded, someone would twist it into knots. Cobb added that it was just such maltreatment that turned him from being a mild-mannered player into a belligerent one.

However, Cobb believed that the way rookies were treated in the 1940s was "gentlemanly." It's interesting, though, that if you'd ask a player from any old era if they were treated well as a rookie, he'd emphatically say "No." So each generation thinks they had it the worst.

Bell Sounds Off

David Bell, a member of the 1998 Seattle Mariners, has baseball roots that go back to the 1950s. His grandfather, Gus, was a major-leaguer, as was his father, Buddy. That makes the Bell family the second of just two three-generation baseball families (the other one is the Boone family, which featured Ray, his son Bob, and grandchildren Aaron and Bret).

At any rate, Bell has a theory about why rookies were treated a lot rougher in the old days. "Maybe guys stayed with a team longer, and they developed more of a close-knit thing where you had to break into their circle." Bell, who once wore a skirt, much to the delight of Cardinal veterans, agrees with the consensus, saying, "Guys are easier on rookies now."

Umpires Also Guilty

Maybe Bell is correct, but Kevin Stocker feels umpires aren't as tolerant of rookies as they are of veterans. He feels that umps don't seem to give first-year players a fair shake. The Devil Rays played Atlanta in a 1998 contest featuring a marquee pitchers' duel. The Braves sent perennial Cy Young winner Greg Maddux to the mound to face rookie sensation Rolando Arrojo, who would shortly be named to the All-Star team.

Said Stocker of the duel, "It's not that simple. It's Maddux and the umpire against Arrojo and the umpire." Translation: The home plate umpire was a different man, or at least he called the game as if he were two different men, depending upon which pitcher was throwing. "Maddux gets another four inches off the plate. It was tough to see Rolando not get calls. You have to realize, this is Maddux; Rolando is a rookie." So, while the double standard apparently does exist, it still seems unfair to poor rookies. But, after all, that is their destiny.

Conclusion

You no longer have to be baffled, imagining what the life of a rookie is like. It has ranged from vicious pranks in the old days to false felony accusations. It has ranged from nearly savage indoctrination into the majors by veterans of the past to relatively mild contemporary treatment (despite still having to pay some dues to umpires). Throughout it all, a rookie season has never been exactly easy. Most rookies have found they can tolerate the high jinks, pranks, and virtually anything else that goes with the territory. Such is the life of a rookie.

Chapter Eight

LAST CHANCE
TO PLAY MANAGER

There's an old joke about the time a manager came to visit a beleaguered pitcher on the mound. The manager had signaled to the bullpen for a much-needed pitching change. The pitcher squawked about the move, saying, "I can get the next guy out. I struck him out the first time I faced him, right?" The manager wearily replied, "Yeah, but that was still back in this inning."

If you've been playing manager, you, too, may be weary, but you have to suck it up for one more inning. To wrap up our journey through the world of baseball, here's one last chance to be baseball's version of an armchair quarterback. Once more, explore baseball strategy and make your calls.

Legal Strategy?

As a big league manager, would you be allowed to move an outfielder into the infield? Or, could you move an infielder and place him in the outfield?

Answer: Sure, and it has been done. (They say this innovation was created by Branch Rickey.) One day in the 1950s, Charlie Dressen was managing for the Brooklyn Dodgers. Leo Durocher was managing the New York Giants. At one point, Leo "The Lip" pinch-hit for his pitcher. He used Artie Wilson, a player Dressen had managed once in the minors. Realizing Wilson was not a pull hitter, Dressen had his right fielder, Carl Furillo, play between second and third base.

Employing a five-man infield made the left side of the diamond resemble an infield shift, another popular tactic (used mostly against dead-pull hitters such as Ted Williams and Willie Stargell).

Wilson failed to hit the ball into the vacant area in right field, grounding out instead. The gamble had worked, and Dressen looked good.

While managing the Reds, Birdie Tebbetts liked to use the five-man infield in obvious bunt situations.

Recent Five-Man Infield Situations

The Chicago Cubs used the five-man infield as recently as August 8, 1998, against the St. Louis Cardinals. The game was tied in the bottom of the 13th inning with nobody out. There were runners on first and third when Mark McGwire swaggered to the plate. At that point, Cubs manager Jim Riggleman made two decisions.

First, he walked McGwire intentionally to set up the force play at every base—most importantly at home plate. Second, with Ray Lankford at the plate, the Cubs brought center fielder Lance Johnson in to play the infield. Mark Grace remained at first and Mickey Morandini stayed at second. Johnson played between Morandini and the second base bag, giving the Cubs three men on the right side of the infield.

Meanwhile, Sammy Sosa moved over from right to right-center and Henry Rodriguez shifted a bit from left to left-center. Despite all the managerial machinations, the Cubs lost. Lankford, who had struck out his first five times before homering in the 11th inning to keep the Cards alive, singled between Morandini and Johnson to cap a wild 9–8 win.

The Cubs repeated this tactic in a crucial situation during the 1998 season finale. Needing a double play, they brought in outfielder Orlando Merced to play a few feet away from second base. A sacrifice fly made it a moot point this time.

Swing Shift

Getting back to the more frequently employed infield shift, it was used against San Diego's Greg Vaughn. The Diamond-backs deployed three men on the left side of the diamond in a game on July 22, 1998. The result? Vaughn homered with two men on, giving him his sixth poke in 9 games. It brought to mind the cliché "You played him deep enough, but not high enough." Vaughn's reaction to the shift was, "I was trying to hit the ball to second base."

Hondo's Walk

As for a four-man outfield, that, too, is perfectly legal. Dave Bristol is supposed to have used it with Cincinnati in the 1960s.

Frank "Hondo" Howard was always an imposing sight at the plate. He stood 6 feet, 7 inches and went about 255 pounds. The strong outfielder simply scorched the ball. While serving as a coach for Tampa Bay, he reminisced about this unusual managerial move. "I have seen managers with a big power hitter up and a one-run lead going into the 9th inning take one infielder out of the infield and put four outfielders out there. I know Birdie Tebbetts did it to keep away from [giving up] a double."

The manager wished to prevent a leadoff two-base hit, since that would put the tying run in scoring position with three cracks still left at knotting the game. He would tolerate a scratch single against his defensive arrangement. Howard was asked who was hitting when Tebbetts made this call, and he replied, "He did it to me."

Another time, Tebbetts placed his shortstop, Roy McMillan, in the outfield to defend against Stan Musial in a situation where Musial's Cardinals needed a long drive to win the game. In that instance, Art Fowler struck out Musial.

You vs. LaRussa

Think back to Tony LaRussa's St. Louis experiment mentioned in the chapter on "Trick Plays." Realize, too, that after using Polanco in the ninth position in the batting order the first day of his innovation, LaRussa had the freedom to use other personnel. For example, in the next 2 games, he hit catcher Tom Pagnozzi ninth. Later, he used Pat Kelly at second base instead of Polanco and hit Kelly ninth as well.

For your data bank, Pagnozzi entered 1998 with a lifetime batting average of .255. He had collected 43 home runs and had driven in 310 runs over 876 big league games. As a catcher, you'd expect him to be a slow runner. At best, he probably ranks as an average runner.

Would he be much help if he got on base, or would he clog up the base paths? Would the next three batters benefit when he got on base, or would there simply be more double plays? Would it be smarter to go with a faster man, such as Kelly?

Answer: While LaRussa didn't stick with Pagnozzi for long (using a variety of players instead), this pitcher-batting-eighth strategy doesn't offer a simple answer. Sorry, no answer this time. In a way, the jury is still out because although the experiment seems to have failed, other managers might employ this tactic in the future. Who knows? You're on your own for this call.

One thing is for sure: LaRussa felt he had to do something to help his slugger. By July 28, McGwire led the majors in intentional walks drawn with 22. That was more than twice as many intentional walks as the American League leader, Ken Griffey, Jr., who had 10.

Further, Big Mac had been walked a total of 102 total times (and ended with a league-record 162 bases on balls). In 1961, when Maris set the home run record, he drew just 94 walks because he had better protection around him in the Yankees' batting order. Pitchers that year were apparently more fearful of pitching to Mickey Mantle (126 walks, best in the majors). In 1998, nobody really wanted to pitch to McGwire, and the St. Louis offense wasn't exactly awe-inspiring.

Now it should also be noted that LaRussa did indeed scrap the McGwire experiment after using his unique lineup just once in spring training of 1999. In 1998 the Cardinals' record with that lineup in effect was 46–36, but LaRussa said it proved to be a distraction. He said he didn't think coaches and managers should be the focus in the media: "...the more they're in the paper, the worse it is. The game is about the players."

He also said the controversial lineup had only one failing. "The only time you get burned, according to somebody that wants to second-guess you, is when you've got the bases loaded and two outs and the eighth-place hitter comes up. Well, yeah, I'd rather have a position player than a pitcher bat there, but there's almost no other [negative] situation."

Well, according to a statistical study, LaRussa was wrong in undertaking this experimental batting order. Instead of giving McGwire more opportunities to drive in runs, "Big Mac" had fewer chances, losing about 20 runs driven in. Thus, the experiment may have cost him the RBI crown in 1998 (he wound up 11 behind leader Sammy Sosa).

By the way, around the time the experiment began, LaRussa said he felt McGwire would break the Maris record in 1998, "if they [opposing pitchers and managers] challenge him to the very end." They did, and he did—easily. Big Mac swatted number 62 on September 8!

As a side note, in 1998 Jack McKeon, manager of the Cincinnati Reds, stated that he had managed a team in the minors that hit a pitcher in the fifth position. The pitcher was Jackie Collum, and the team was the Triple-A Vancouver squad back in 1962. In McKeon's case, he batted the pitcher that high simply because the team's offense was so weak. McKeon said he even used Collum as his number-one pinch hitter.

Triple Steal

Is there actually such a thing as a triple steal? If so, would any manager conceive of trying it?

Answer: Sure there is such a thing. In fact, on July 25 in 1930, Connie Mack's Philadelphia Athletics pulled this play off successfully in the 1st inning against the Indians. What made that game truly noteworthy, though, was the fact that in the 4th inning Mack's Athletics ran the play again. Once more it worked!

Now, if you're thinking, "Sure, that was an era when teams scraped for runs and did anything they could to eke out a win," you are 100 percent wrong. The 1930 season produced perhaps the most explosive offensive in baseball history. For example, six of the eight teams in the National League hit over .300. As a matter of fact, the league had a composite batting average of .303! Never before or since has an entire league topped the .300 plateau. The Phillies hit .315, yet lost 102 games to finish in the basement due to a miserable team ERA of 6.71. Even the .319 (first in the N.L.) team average of the Giants couldn't take them to a pennant.

In addition, Bill Terry hit .401. He was the last National Leaguer to top the coveted .400 plateau. Hack Wilson had his 56 HR, 191 RBI season that year. Finally, the collective ERA of the National League was an inflated 4.97—so, runs were hardly scarce that season.

Standard Procedure

Here's one to test your understanding of what managers always do in a volatile situation. To set the stage, let's say it's the bottom of the ninth in a tie game. With one out, the home team has a runner on third. As the manager of the team out in the field, what special alignment would your outfielders be in? (The question refers to the depth of the outfielders.)

Answer: Just as a manager will have his infield play in when he wants them to cut down a run at the plate in certain circumstances, in our scenario the outfield, too, must be shallow. Each outfielder knows how strong or weak his arm is and will play accordingly. A man like Larry Walker could be a bit deeper than a Juan Gonzalez.

No matter how strong the hitter, the outfield won't be very deep. After all, what good is it to catch a deep blast off the bat of an opposing slugger for out number two if the runner on third is going to tag to win the game? So, you must play at a depth where you have a chance to gun down the runner. Another advantage is that an outfielder who has come in some will be able to catch a sinking line drive that would've fallen in otherwise. No run will score on such a play, and you'll record a big out.

Rule of Thumb (or of Legs)

Imagine you are the Oakland A's manager during Rickey Henderson's prime years (circa 1982, when he stole a sizzling all-time record of 130 bases). Henderson is on second with two outs in a scoreless game. Would you allow him to swipe third? What's the rule of thumb about stealing third with two outs?

Answer: Whether you would allow Henderson to take off for third is one matter. Perhaps because he is so special, you, as an aggressive manager, might let him take the risk. The important factor here, though, is the seldom-broken rule that says you don't steal third with two outs. Actually, the logic dictates you steal third only in a one-out situation.

The reasons why you do this have been well thought out. After all, with nobody out, your team will still have three cracks at bringing home the runner who is already in scoring position. You could even sacrifice a runner over and still have two chances to score on a hit or, for example, a sacrifice fly. Therefore, why risk the steal with nobody out?

With two outs, going to third isn't a big advantage over what you already have: a runner perched in scoring position. In other words, most hits that would score the man from third would also score him from second because the runner will take off at the crack of the bat with two down. Furthermore, with two outs you can't score from third on a sac fly anyway.

Being at third instead of second allows you to score only on something like a wild pitch or passed ball.

One huge advantage of stealing third with one out is that the batter can then drive the runner in with a sacrifice fly (or perhaps a groundout). It's rare to try to steal third unless there's one out. The corollary to the "rule" about stealing third is that the base runner should never make the first or the third out of the inning trying to go to third. Good runners know that with no outs or with two outs it doesn't make sense to, say, try to make it from first to third on a single, unless there is virtually no doubt that they can make it.

When to Scoot to Third

Big league managers don't have to worry about routine items such as the last example, which was routine albeit on a higher level. However, we're still going to make you prove that you know your stuff with an easy question. When does a runner on second base try to advance to third on a ground ball that appears to be headed for an infielder? Do you go on balls hit to the left side or to the right? Is there a rule of thumb here?

Answer: The broad rule is a runner goes immediately if the ball is hit to the right side of the diamond. On balls hit to the left side, the runner almost always holds second. And yet, if it is hit slowly, hit on a very high chop, or hit somewhat up the middle, a good runner *can* make it to third. One coach said he taught his players that if the ball was hit to the shortstop in a position where he has to go up the middle and is running away from third, then the runner can make it to third. Many things, especially the speed of the runner and the ability of the shortstop, must be considered as well.

To Squeeze or Not to Squeeze

Do managers squeeze with a lefty in the batter's box, or is that considered poor strategy?

Answer: It's not poor strategy. Wade Boggs said, "I think if they're a good bunter, it doesn't matter if they're left-handed or right-handed. Kevin Stocker's a switch hitter and we've squeezed with him batting left-handed. If the runner does his part at third base and gets a late enough break so the pitcher doesn't dictate [the play], all you have to do is put the ball down, and the runner scores anyway."

Bobby Cox agrees, "We do it all the time with [southpaw pitcher] Tom Glavine. If you can get the bunt down, I know the catcher has a clear look at the runner and all that, but that doesn't make any difference. As long as the guy doesn't leave early, you're in good shape."

Squeeze Against Lefty/Righty?

Is it more advantageous to squeeze against a left-handed pitcher, a righty, or is there no difference?

Answer: According to Boggs, it doesn't make any difference. Out of the stretch position, a lefty is looking toward first while a righty is facing the runner on third. Some fans think that's a factor. Boggs stated that with any pitcher, "by the time he comes up, turns, focuses towards home, and gets ready to throw the ball, then if you break [from third], it's just timing."

Stocker goes along with Boggs, adding, "If you run it at the major league level, and you run it right, nobody will know [the play is on] except the third baseman, because he can see the runner take off, but by then it shouldn't matter."

Prevent the Squeeze?

If the runner on third tips off the squeeze play, would a manager ever have the pitcher deliberately hit the batter? By hitting the batter, the ball is dead, and the runner must return to third. Would a manager advocate this?

Answer: It depends on whom you listen to, but we think he would. Stocker said, "They're not going to throw at you to hit you; they're going to throw it high and tight or up and away—trying to get you to foul it off. They might try to throw it in the dirt.

"The goal is not so much to try to hit you or get an out.

The goal is to try to get you to bunt it foul or miss the ball," he concluded. Of course if you miss the ball, the result is an out. If you pitch the batter high, and he bunts a pop-up, you could get a double play.

Now, if you ask Bobby Cox if you should hit a batter, he'd reply, "I think you would. At least throw it at him." He also said the other option was to throw it way outside. "You'll do one or the other if you smell it—if he's coming way down the line too early. You'd better do it [hit him] to save a game. If you read it, you've got to adjust. You're not going to hurt anybody, I'm just saying, to stop the play you damn near gotta do it."

He said that to come in "high and tight is what you should do, knock him down, and the catcher's got the ball. If it hits him, it hits him." He viewed such a tactic as being, in effect, "the same thing as a pitchout."

More Squeeze Play Notes

In 1969, Johnny Goryl coached in Minnesota with Billy Martin, the last manager who used the safety squeeze to any real extent. Goryl said, "Billy's favorite play was runners at first and third with one out, and he'd have [his hitters such as] Ted Uhlaender or Richie Reese drag the ball between the pitcher and the first baseman to steal a run that way.

"And if the first baseman wasn't alert, we might end up with runners on first and second, but it was really to squeeze out a run. It's a weapon to use when you want to add to a lead."

Leyland's Squeeze

Goryl added that nowadays, "Jim Leyland would be one person who would make use of a weapon like that depending on what kind of ball club he's got, where he's at in the batting order and the count, and if the batter's swinging good at the time. All those factors enter into running the squeeze."

More Thoughts on Squeezing

In 1998, a year of tremendous offensive punch in baseball, Scott Brosius offered his view of why squeeze plays aren't used too often. "The way runs are being scored right now, with a lot of the hitters being bigger and stronger, the managers feel that they have a better chance of driving them in from third base instead of bunting them in," said Brosius. "With less than two outs, a lot of the players have a better chance of hitting the ball to the outfield [for a sacrifice fly]."

Chris Chambliss tends to dislike trick plays; he prefers to stick to the basics. He said, "Baseball is a game that does take a lot of doing different things to get your offense rolling sometimes, but we all know what those things are. And you kinda work within your own personnel. If you have guys who hit a lot of home runs, you may not want to be trying all those kind of plays."

Conclusion

Perhaps Chambliss is correct. Yet, if you're a gambling kind of manager, this chapter gave you a chance to be bold. Of course, if you were actually getting paid to manage a big league team, you might be a tad more conservative and play it by the book. Face it, few managers can play the game like the respected, successful Cox, who said there is no book.

Most managers live and die by the mythical, but respected and feared "book." The repercussions for going against it are great. Couch-potato managers have the liberty of throwing that book out their den windows.

INDEX

Aaron, Hank, 11, 17, 22, 25, 64
Abbott, Glenn, 7
Adcock, Joe, 64–65
Agnew, Sam, 19
Alexander, Grover, 16
Allen, Dick, 54
Alomar, Roberto, 27
Alomar, Sandy, 47, 49
Alvarez, Wilson, 70, 77, 78
Anderson, Brian, 47
Anderson, Sparky, 43–46, 55
Arizona Diamond-backs, 48, 83
Arrojo, Rolando, 80
Atlanta Braves, 20, 23–24, 36, 38, 43, 46, 77, 80
Ausmus, Brad, 37

Baker, Dusty, 8, 9
Baltimore Orioles, 27, 29, 30–31, 39, 45, 70–71
Barrow, Ed, 19

Bavasi, Buzzi, 57
Baylor, Don, 43, 53
Bell, Buddy, 79
Bell, David, 79–80
Bell, Gus, 79
Belle, Albert, 31
Bench, Johnny, 49
Bender, Chief, 63
Berra, Yogi, 17, 57
Bevington, Terry, 55

Bichette, Dante, 56, 57
Blass, Steve, 74
Blue, Vida, 7
Blyleven, Bert, 57
Bogar, Tim, 33–343
Boggs, Wade, 20, 66–67, 77, 89–90
Bonds, Barry, 8, 9, 26
Bones, Ricky, 47
Boone, Aaron, 79
Boone, Bob, 79
Boone, Bret, 79
Boone, Ray, 79
Borders, Pat, 47
Boston Red Sox, 12, 19, 33, 65
Brede, Brent, 8
Brett, George, 55
Bristol, Dave, 83
Brock, Lou, 37
Brooklyn Dodgers, 18, 38, 82
Brosius, Scott, 78, 92
Buckner, Bill, 38
Buford, Damon, 29
Buhner, Jay, 18
Bumbry, Al, 39
Busch, August, 58
Bush, Joe, 68
Buynak, Cy, 73

California Angels, 30
Candiotti, Tom, 35
Canseco, Jose, 27
Carlton, Steve, 50, 56, 62
Carter, Gary, 43
Castillo, Marty, 33
Cavaretta, Phil, 5

Cedeno, Cesar, 38
Chambliss, Chris, 41, 45, 78, 79, 92
Chicago Cubs, 5, 7, 9–10, 17, 37, 40, 42, 60, 82, 83
Chicago White Sox, 10, 36, 54, 70, 78
Cincinnati Reds, 7, 53, 63, 82, 83, 86
Clark, Jack, 13–14
Clark, Will, 27
Clemente, Roberto, 34
Cleveland Indians, 27, 33, 46, 49–50, 62, 72, 73, 77, 88
Clyde, David, 69–70
Cobb, Ty, 19–20, 79
Coleman, Vince, 37
Collum, Jackie, 86
Colorado Rockies, 6, 34, 48
Comiskey Park, 54
Cone, David, 76
Conigliaro, Tony, 58
Corrales, Pat, 36–37, 46, 77
Cosgrove, Mike, 7
Cox, Bobby, 20, 43, 90–91
Cromartie, Warren, 28

Dark, Alvin, 7
Dauer, Rich, 47
Davis, Chili, 50
Davis, Gerry, 36

Dean, Dizzy, 18, 54, 59
DeShields, Delino, 8
Detroit Tigers, 33, 36, 44, 65
Dickey, Bill, 60
Dierker, Larry, 32
Dietz, Dick, 30
DiMaggio, Joe, 60
Dorish, Harry, 45
Dressen, Charlie, 53, 82
Dressendorfer, Kirk, 72–73
Drysdale, Don, 18, 30
Duncan, Dave, 73
Durham, Ray, 36–37
Durocher, Leo, 53, 82

Eckersley, Dennis, 66

Fernandez, Sid, 35–36
Fetters, Mike, 52
Fidrych, Mark, 69–70
Fingers, Rollie, 7
Flaherty, John, 44–45
Flannagan, Mike, 58
Florida Marlins, 78
Fowler, Art, 84
Foxx, Jimmie, 12
Frey, Jim, 55
Fryman, Travis, 43, 49
Furillo, Carl, 82

Gaetti, Gary, 54
Galvin, Pud, 61
Gant, Ron, 8

Gehrig, Lou, 15, 60, 68

Giambi, Jason, 52

Gibson, Bob, 56, 65

Glavine, Tom, 90

Gomez, Lefty, 58

Gomez, Preston, 6, 7

Gonzalez, Juan, 87

Gooden, Dwight, 17, 42, 76

Goosen, Greg, 56

Goryl, Johnny, 43, 44, 45–46, 48, 91

Grace, Mark, 82–83

Graffanino, Tony, 38

Granger, Jeff, 74

Griffey, Ken Jr., 21–22, 75, 85

Griffith, Clark, 10

Grimes, Burleigh, 25

Guillen, Jose, 74, 34

Haddix, Harvey, 64

Hansen, Jed, 47

Hargrove, Mike, 72

Harnisch, Pete, 77

Harper, Terry, 23–24

Harrah, Toby, 56

Harrelson, Bud, 50

Harris, Greg, 63

Harwell, Ernie, 36

Head, Ed, 63

Henderson, Rickey, 88

Henry, Doug, 36

Hershiser, Orel, 9, 13

Herzog, Whitey, 55, 58

Hoak, Don, 64

Holloman, Alva, 61

Horlen, Joe, 58

Horner, Bob, 59

Hornsby, Rogers, 16–17

Houston Astrodome, 33

Houston Astros, 7, 32, 33, 36, 38

Howard, Frank, 10, 44, 83

Howe, Art, 52

Hrabosky, Al, 30–31

Huggins, Miller, 15, 16

Hunter, Brian, 14

Hurst, Bruce, 33

Ireland, Tim, 48–49

Jackson, Reggie, 56, 57

Jeter, Derek, 50

John, Tommy, 37–38

Johnson, Lance, 82–83

Johnson, Walter, 61

Johnstone, Jay, 71

Jones, Andruw, 38

Jordan, Brian, 51

Kansas City Royals, 47, 55

Kelly, Pat, 84

Kirby, Clay, 6, 7

Klein, Chuck, 11

Knight, Ray, 53

Knowles, Darold, 57

Kranepool, Ed, 56

Kruk, John, 57

Kuiper, Duane, 73

Lajoie, Nap, 10

Lankford, Ray, 9, 51, 82

LaRussa, Tony, 50–51, 84–86

Lasorda, Tommy, 13–14, 72

Lazzeri, Tony, 60

Lefebvre, Jim, 38

Leyland, Jim, 91

Lindblad, Paul, 7

Los Angeles Dodgers, 10, 12–13, 28, 30, 35

Louisville, 22

Mack, Connie, 86

Maddux, Greg, 80

Mantilla, Felix, 64

Mantle, Mickey, 36, 85

Manwaring, Kirt, 34

Maris, Roger, 51, 85

Martin, Billy, 40, 91

Martinez, Dennis, 38, 49–50

Martinez, Pedro, 65

Mathewson, Christy, 63

Mauch, Gene, 55

Mayne, Brent, 8

Mays, Carl, 68

McCarver, Tim, 56

McClendon, Lloyd, 42

McCovey, Willie, 11

McCracken, Quinton, 77

McCray, Rodney, 22–23

McDowell, Sam, 46

Macfarlane, Mike, 52

McGee, Willie, 9, 37

McGillicuddy,

Cornelius, 87–88

McGinnity, Joe, 63

McGraw, Tug, 56

McGwire, Mark, 8–9, 52, 57, 82, 85–86

McKeon, Jack, 86

McLain, Denny, 65

McMillan, Roy, 84

Merced, Orlando, 83

Miller, Ray, 31, 45, 68

Milwaukee Braves, 64

Milwaukee Brewers, 52, 55

Monahan, Shane, 75

Monday, Rick, 28

Montgomery, Bob, 41

Montreal Expos, 28, 42, 63, 65

Morandini, Mickey, 82–83

Muesel, Bob, 15

Musial, Stan, 84

Nen, Robb, 9

New York Giants, 63, 88

New York Mets, 6, 76

New York Yankees, 15, 26, 37–48, 40, 41, 45, 46, 60, 78

Nicholson, Bill, 9–10

Niedenfuer, Tom, 13

Oakland Athletics, 7, 49–50, 52, 72–73, 88

O'Farrell, Bob, 16

Olereud, John, 50

Orosco, Jesse, 75–76

Ott, Mel, 9–10, 11

Owen, Spike, 49

Pagnozzi, Tom, 84–85

Paige, Satchel, 53

Palmeiro, Rafael, 42, 78

Pappas, Erik, 71

Patek, Fred, 74

Pelekoudas, Chris, 22

Pena, Tony, 49–50, 52

Percival, Troy, 30–31

Perez, Neifi, 48

Perez, Tony, 7

Perry, Gaylord, 32, 64

Perry, Herbert, 77

Peterson, Fritz, 73

Philadelphia Athletics, 63, 86–87

Philadelphia Phillies, 11, 50, 62, 88

Piazza, Mike, 35

Pierce, Billy, 45

Pittsburgh Pirates, 23, 34, 38, 57, 64, 74

Polanco, Placido, 50, 84–85

Polo Grounds, 10

Poole, Jim, 8, 9

Pruett, Hub, 10

Ramirez, Alex, 72

Ramirez, Manny, 33–34, 73

Reese, Richie, 91

Reliford, Charlie, 33–34

Remy, Jerry, 33, 66

Richards, Gene, 23–24

Richards, Paul, 45

Rickey, Branch, 82

Riggleman, Jim, 82

Rivers, Ruben, 52

Roberts, Bip, 65

Robinson, Jackie, 20

Rodgers, Buck, 42

Rodriguez, Felix, 48

Rodriguez, Henry, 83

Rojas, Mel, 65

Rothschild, Larry, 40, 43

Ruth, Babe, 10, 15–16, 18–19, 25, 54, 68, 70–71

Ryan, Nolan, 17, 18

St. Louis Cardinals, 9, 13, 15, 22, 37, 58, 65, 80, 82, 84–86

Sanders, Deion, 56–57

San Diego Padres, 6, 23–24, 35, 52, 83

San Francisco Giants, 8–9, 10, 11

Score, Herb, 29

Seattle Mariners, 21–22, 75, 79

Selkirk, George, 60

Sewell, Joe, 62

Shooton, Burt, 11

Showalter, Buck, 8

Simmons, Curt, 22

Slaught, Don, 26, 37–38

Smith, Ozzie, 13

Sosa, Sammy, 86

Spahn, Warren, 45

Sportsman's Park, 22

Springstead, Marty, 59

Stargell, Willie, 82

Staub, Rusty, 32

Stengel, Casey, 53, 57

Stocker, Kevin, 20, 46–47, 80, 89–91

Stottlemyre, Todd, 50

Sutcliffe, Rick, 15, 71

Sweeney, Mark, 52

Tampa Bay Devil Rays, 20, 40, 66–67, 77, 80, 83–84

Tavares, Julian, 73

Tebbetts, Birdie, 82, 84

Tekulve, Kent, 46

Terry, Bill, 87

Texas Rangers, 27, 69

Thomas, Darrell, 35

Thome, Jim, 73

Thompson, Ryan, 76

Three Rivers Stadium, 23

Torre, Joe, 40, 41, 45, 55

Torrez, Mike, 66

Trebelhorn, Tom, 55

Trillo, Manny, 42–43

Turner, Ted, 55

Uecker, Bob, 54

Uhlaender, Ted, 91

Vancouver, 86

Van Slyke, Andy, 14

Vargo, Ed, 24

Vaughn, Greg, 83

Vaughn, Mo, 29–30

Ventura, Robin, 78

Wagner, Honus, 68

Walker, Larry, 87

Ward, Turner, 23, 38

Washington Senators, 10

Weaver, Earl, 39–40, 53, 59

Wendelstedt, Harry, 30

Williams, Bernie, 26

Williams, Dick, 71

Williams, Matt, 47–48

Williams, Ted, 82

Wilson, Artie, 82

Wilson, Don, 7

Wilson, Glenn, 57

Wilson, Hack, 60, 87

Winfield, Dave, 38, 35

Wrigley, Phil, 5

Wrigley Field, 54, 57, 74

Wrong-Way Corrigan, 35–36

Wynn, Early, 18

Yankee Stadium, 36, 58

Yastrzemski, Carl, 65, 66

Young, Cy, 15, 61, 62, 71, 80

Young, Matt, 29

Zimmer, Don, 40–43

ABOUT THE AUTHOR

Wayne Stewart spent the first twenty-one years of his life in Donora, Pennsylvania. That same small town produced a handful of big league baseball players including Ken Griffey, Sr., one of Wayne's high school classmates. Donora is also the birthplace of Hall-of-Famer Stan "The Man" Musial and potential future Hall of Fame outfielder Ken Griffey, Jr. (coincidentally, both born on November 21).

Stewart now lives in Lorain, Ohio. He is married to Nancy (Panich) Stewart and is the father of Sean and Scott. He has been writing professionally for over twenty years and has sold over 500 articles to national publications such as *Baseball Digest*, Beckett Publications, *USA Today/Baseball Weekly*, and *Boys' Life*.

His first book, *Baseball Oddities*, was published by Sterling in 1998. Stewart has written stories for many team publications including the Braves, Yankees, White Sox, Orioles, Padres, Twins, Phillies, Red Sox, A's, and Dodgers. In addition, he is a member of S.A.B.R. (Society for American Baseball Research) and has written for one of their prestigious publications, *Baseball Research Journal*.

He has also appeared in several Spring editions of baseball magazines out of New York, and in four newspapers in the Cleveland area. Additionally, he has written for *Sports Heritage* and *The Minneapolis Review*. He even hosted several sports shows (including a call-in program) on a local radio station.

Stewart has taught English in Lorain City Schools for over 25 years. Currently, he is working at Whittier Middle School.